On Ret

This new series, published by Medio Media/Arthur James, responds to the spiritual needs of people living today's busy and stressed lifestyle. Each book in the series is designed to allow the reader to develop a space for silence and solitude and spiritual practice in the context of ordinary life or by taking a short period of withdrawal. The structure of the book allows a flexible timetable to be constructed which integrates periods of reading, physical practice or exercise, and meditation.

Laurence Freeman is a Benedictine monk of the Monastery of Christ the King in London and Director of the World Community for Christian Meditation. He was a student of John Main and succeeded him in the work of teaching meditation in the Christian tradition as a way to strengthen the unity and peace between all peoples and faiths. He writes and travels to teach and to serve in the community that grows from meditation.

Also in the 'On Retreat With ...' Series

SELF AND ENVIRONMENT
Charles Bran[illegible]

THE MY[illegible]ERY BEYOND
Bede Griffiths

AWAKENING
John Main

SILENT WISDOM, HIDDEN LIGHT
Eileen O'Hea

Other books by Laurence Freeman

LIGHT WITHIN

THE SELFLESS SELF

A SHORT SPAN OF DAYS

CHRISTIAN MEDITATION: YOUR DAILY PRACTICE

WEB OF SILENCE

The 'On Retreat With ...' Series

ASPECTS OF LOVE

On Retreat With

Laurence Freeman OSB

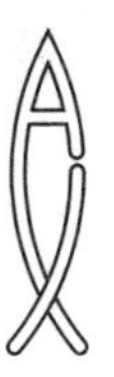

MEDIO MEDIA / ARTHUR JAMES

LONDON AND BERKHAMSTED

First published in Great Britain in 1997 by

MEDIO MEDIA LTD
in association with
ARTHUR JAMES LTD
70 Cross Oak Road
Berkhamsted
Hertfordshire HP4 3HZ

A catalogue record for this book is available
from the British Library.

ISBN 0 85305 423 1

Typeset in Monotype Bulmer by
Strathmore Publishing Services, London N7

Printed and bound in Great Britain by
Guernsey Press Ltd, Guernsey, C.I.

For

Polly and Mark,

Julian, Dominic, and Adrian

Aspects of Love was originally given as a retreat in Montreal in 1996. The retreat is also published in a cassette series by Medio Media.

I am very grateful to Gregory Ryan, whose careful editing of the original retreat has made this book possible. He would not have been able to do this without the elegant transcription of the tapes undertaken by Sadie Summers.

Laurence Freeman

Contents

Being on retreat: how to do it yourself

> Stay in your cell and your cell will teach you everything.
>
> – Saying of the Desert Fathers

> The problems of the world arise from people's inability to sit still in their own room.
>
> – Pascal, *Pensées*

Why set aside time for retreat?

Nature believes in retreats. Each day we virtually shut down our active processes of mind and body for the retreat and renewal we call sleep. Each year the animal and vegetable worlds go through periods of deep rest we call hibernation. These are not escapes from reality but ways of becoming more deeply attuned to reality, respecting its ways and trusting the inherent wisdom of nature.

Between each breath there is a moment of cessation, of deep stillness, which is not the stillness of inaction but the stillness of non-action. Between periods of daily work we naturally trust the mind and body when they tell us to rest. Between two thoughts there is an instant of mental silence.

On the London Underground, many stations have a recorded announcement each time the train stops, warning passengers stepping from the train to the platform to 'mind the gap'. Minding the gap is what this book is about – helping you, we hope, to see and respect the natural human need to retreat from action and speech at set times so that we can return to speech and action refreshed, re-balanced and renewed.

The spiritual life is not a specialized part of daily life. Everything you do in the day, from washing to eating breakfast, having meetings, driving to work, solving problems, making more problems for yourself once you have solved them, watching television or deciding instead to read, going to a restaurant or a movie or going to church, *everything* you do is your spiritual life. It is only a matter of how consciously you do these ordinary things, how attentive you are to the opportunities they offer for growth, for enjoyment, and how mindfully, how selflessly, how compassionately you perform them. Yet to live life spiritually all the time everyone needs to take specific times to focus on the spiritual dimension before everything else.

'Set your mind on God's kingdom and his justice before everything else, and all the rest will come to you as well.' Jesus said this in his Sermon on the Mount (Matt. 6:33). Taking a time of retreat will help you discover what he means by 'kingdom' and 'justice'. It will teach you that the kingdom is not a place but an experience of presence. The kingdom is within us and all around us. And you will learn that justice means balance, harmony, order. We hunger for justice in all the activities and relationships of our lives.

Buddhists see the spiritual significance of daily life in terms of ordinary mindfulness: doing everything with awareness, wakefulness. Christians similarly have long worked at praying at all times, giving glory to God in everything they do, practising the presence of God. This does not mean going around muttering prayers to yourself all day. You would only be more distracted in what you are doing. Nor does it mean thinking about God all the time. That would make you a religious fanatic. Praying ceaselessly, practising the divine presence is not something extra we do but the way we do whatever we are doing. It is a way of *being* in the midst of action: of being-in-action.

Perhaps the best comparison is with a relationship with someone you love. The awareness, the mindfulness, of that love surrounds and permeates you and all your words and responses all the day. You do not have to be thinking of the person you love all the time but they are with you and their often silent presence transforms your consciousness. Yet at the end of the day, or whenever opportunity allows, you return to the full presence of that person. Being with them helps the relationship to grow and deepen, even when romance wears thin. The 'quality times' together are essential for the health and development of love.

How to set up a retreat

The 'On Retreat With …' series has been prepared to help you to spend quality time in the most fundamental relationship of your life, your relationship with God. In the ground of this relationship are planted all your human relationships, even your relationship with yourself. Quality time with someone requires a certain degree of exclusivity – you say *no* to other invitations and pleasant opportunities in order to concentrate on your presence with one person. Other jobs and responsibilities go on hold. When you return to address them you will be refreshed, calmer, and you can see the problems that easily overwhelm you in a better perspective. Retreat is not escape. You make a retreat in order to address reality more realistically and courageously. Retreat does not solve your problems but it helps you deal with them in a more peaceful and hopeful way. This is the meaning of a retreat: we retreat in order to advance deeper into the mystery of love's reality.

This book can help you structure your time and set the tone for the period of retreat you are allowing yourself to take. As life today is very busy and as it often seems impossible to find time for silence, stillness, and non-action, we need all the help we can get in order to take the time of spiritual retreat which both spiritual and psychological health require.

Time and place: your cell

You do not need to take a great stretch of time to make a retreat. But you need to designate a certain period of time and stick to it. It could be an hour, a morning or afternoon, a day, a weekend, a week, three months. In some traditions five-year retreats are customary. Let's start with a couple of hours.

If it is a short time, a couple of hours, you will probably be at home. Or you may have found you have some free time when away on holiday or a business trip. You do not have to fill in the empty space in the agenda: keep it empty. Go into the emptiness and you will emerge refreshed, more fulfilled. Set the time realistically. Put your answer-phone on. Turn the television or radio off. If you need to tell someone not to disturb you for the next couple of hours, do so. Put your work away or walk away from it. Then make a space.

The early Christian monks who lived much in solitude each had a cell. A monastic cell is different from a prison cell: you choose to be there. It is a place of stability, of security, of focus. It does not have to be elaborate. Cells are simple places. A chair, a cushion on the floor, a corner of a room. Make it tidy and clean. Set up a symbol of the presence; this could be a candle – ancient symbol of the presence of Christ – a flower, an icon, a photo, a cross, a Bible, or a simple everyday object. There should be a sense of simplicity, not clutter – of beauty, not prettiness. Have a watch or clock with a timer device nearby (not a loud ticker or too prominently placed).

With steadiness and ease: your body

Your retreat is a homecoming, an integrating, a remembering. It is not a spacewalk or a mind trip. You cannot come home unless you come inside, so take time to consider that you are also taking time to *make friends with your body*. And remember that you are only singling out the body for the purpose of the retreat. In fact you are really one single-woven tapestry of body–mind soaked and grounded in spirit: one being, fully alive.

Single out the body, then, and learn that it is happy to carry you, support you, hug you. It rejoices to pump blood, breathe, digest, walk, and sleep. It is a wonderful, mystical, funny contraption in which we are incarnated, and have epiphanies and transfigurations, and are crucified and resurrected.

Whatever you do on this retreat, keep breathing. Breathe as you take breakfast, as you go for a solitary walk or do some housework in your cell. Breathe while you are on the toilet. Breathe during your spiritual reading and as you doze off to a peaceful sleep after your day of silence.

You already have the three things necessary with which to make friends with your body. They are breath, gravity, and ground. You have been breathing since you were born and you will keep doing so as long as you need to. So relax and let breath breathe you. It is closer to you than your thinking. The way you breathe determines how you feel (see how your breathing changes when you are angry, frightened, or peaceful). As you give your attention to your breath you become naturally heavy. That is gravity hugging you. Give to it. Let it take you to the ground which stands under you (*understands you*). The ground comes up to hold you, so relax and do nothing. In fact, un-do. Let it. You just pay attention to the breath as it breathes you in and out, in and out.

You might enjoy lying on your back before and/or after your meditation times, or after a walk. Lying on your back is an excellent way to start making friends with your body on this retreat. It helps turn off all the tapes playing in your head: tapes telling you to make a good impression on others, to be demure or macho, how to look sexy or respectable, how to dominate and be noticed. When you lie down, the three bony boxes of your body – the head, chest, and pelvis – stop chattering to each other for a while and relate directly to the ground instead. It is like turning gravity off for a moment.

Lie on your back with your knees bent so that your lower back is quite flat on the floor. Let your chin drop lightly towards your chest so that it is no longer pointing up to the ceiling. If this is difficult, put a folded blanket under your head, just an inch or so, no more. And stay, and wait in silence or listen to a taped talk on meditation or some music. If you doze off, so be it. When you do get up, first roll over gently on to your hands and knees. It is not helpful to yank the head straightaway in order to get up, because that immediately undoes all the work that breath, gravity, and ground have just accomplished in straightening you out and unknotting you.

If you want to take this friendship with your body further, you could read *Awakening the Spine* by Vanda Scaravelli, *Yoga Over 50* by Mary Stewart (even if you are 25), and *Yoga and You* by Esther Myers. These three women are yoga teachers of great depth, humour, and insight.

Lectio: your mind and its emotions

Then, sitting comfortably, read a section of this book. Read slowly. The book will last a long time, longer probably than your body. So there is no need to speed-read or devour the book and get on to another one. Re-read what you have read. Let your mind settle on a part of the passage which speaks to you most deeply. This may be just a phrase, a word, an image, or an idea. Revolve around that for a while. You don't have to analyse it. Savour it. The early desert monks called this *lectio*, spiritual (rather than mental) reading.

After a period of *lectio*, which can be ten or fifteen minutes, transfer your attention to the symbol which is the focal point for your retreat-space. Let your attention move towards the symbol, into the presence in the symbol. Let thought relax and the mind be still. When thoughts, fantasies, fears, anxieties, restlessness surface, let them come and let them go. Say, 'I'm sorry, you'll have to come and see me later. I'm busy doing nothing at the moment.' They will get the message if you give it strongly; be ruthless with them and don't compromise.

Meditation: going deeper

This would be a good time now for your meditation. Depending on how long you have been meditating or if you are just beginning, decide how many periods of meditation you are going to have during your retreat. A minimum would be two a day. Don't overdo it, but if you are a regular meditator you can profitably put additional periods in. More is not automatically better, of course. Three would be moderate. Six periods would be fine if you were sure you were not straining yourself or getting greedy.

Sit down with your back straight, sit still, close your eyes. Take a few deep breaths and then breathe normally. Then, silently, begin to repeat your word, your mantra. A good Christian mantra is the word *maranatha*. It means, 'Come, Lord,' or, 'The Lord comes,' but do not think of its meaning as you say it. Say the word simply and listen to it as you say it. This is the journey of faith, the deep listening. Faith leads to love. You could also take the word *Jesus* or *abba* (an Aramaic word used by Jesus, meaning 'father'). Whatever word you choose, stay with the same word throughout the meditation (and from one meditation period to the next) so that it can progressively take you deeper, from mind to heart.

Do not say the word with force. You are not trying to blank out the mind. Do not fight the thoughts which will come to you from every direction. Keep returning to the mantra. Say the word from the beginning to the end of the meditation whether you are aware of feeling distracted or peaceful. As soon as you realize you have stopped saying the word, start saying it again. In time (anywhere between five minutes and twenty years) the mantra will lead you at moments into complete stillness and silence, beyond itself. But if you are conscious of being silent then you are not yet completely silent, so keep on saying the mantra until the Spirit takes over. You will find that you say the mantra more deeply, more finely, more delicately as time goes on. Time your meditation with a timer – not too alarming a sound. If you are new to meditation, begin with twenty minutes (or less if you really find twenty too long). Otherwise thirty minutes is a good period to meditate for. If you have a gong, this will help lead into and out of the meditation peacefully.

After the meditation, come out slowly. Open your eyes. Pay attention to the symbol you have set up in front of you. This would be a good time to read some scripture. *The Burning Heart* would be a good book to use at this point – a collection of John Main's favourite Scripture passages with a short commentary by him. Again, read slowly, chewing and savouring the Word. Don't gulp it down. You could then listen to some music, do some yoga, draw, or paint.

Structuring your time of retreat

If you have to get back to work and daily life, take a few moments to appreciate the gift of present you have just enjoyed – let it go, be non-possessive. Read another section of this book, again slowly and savouring what appeals to you. Open yourself to the next thing you have to do and prepare to do it while keeping your mind and heart open to the presence you have just turned towards. Your prayerfulness continues into whatever you are now going to do. And you can share the fruits of peace and joy you have received with others, not by preaching, but in the way you relate to them. If you need to, pack up your retreat things reverently and get on with life.

If you have more time you can vary the elements of this retreat time. If you have a whole day, for example, you could schedule two, three, or four meditations. This will depend somewhat on your experience in meditation. Don't overdo it, and more does not mean better. If you are making the retreat with others, that will introduce another dimension of presence. Use this book together, reading it aloud. If you have a weekend or even longer you will need to schedule your time more carefully. Draw up a timetable but allow yourself to be flexible in keeping to it. Morning, midday, and evening are natural times for prayer – and before you go to bed. If you have a day or longer on retreat, do some manual work, even housecleaning, and get some exercise and fresh air. Walk in the garden or a park. Take this book with you and stop and read a section during your walk.

Don't just do something, sit there!

You might find the voice of conscience attacking you during your retreat. 'You are wasting your time,' it will say, or, 'You are being selfish.' You will think of all the practical, urgent, problematic things you could do. You will get an insight into a situation and want to dash off to implement it. Watch these restless thoughts and they will die down and return less frequently. This is why you will benefit from scheduling your time. It will fool your bush mind into thinking you are doing something productive. But your heart will teach you that you are not trying to produce or achieve anything. You are being. You are drinking deep, in the desert of modern life, of the waters of divine being. Your work and the people you live with, will all benefit from this time of retreat, so you are not being selfish. A gentle discipline in ordering your time of retreat – whether an hour or a day or a weekend – will help awaken a sense of inner freedom from anxiety, obsession, and fear. Enjoy it: find joy in it.

Laurence Freeman

'In the light of the experience of meditation we are able to see the balance of love in our life, the great balancing power of love that creates us, that accompanies us throughout our life, that heals and teaches us.'

– John Main

Part One

Homecoming

Recently, while visiting some meditators, I saw a wonderful sight that is so welcome: the Canada geese returning home, a sign of the end of winter. In the fall, the Canada geese go south, obeying the law of migration and giving humanity another sign of nature being true to itself. Those geese are simply being true to their own nature and their deepest instinct to *come home*. One of the things that the sight gave me was the sense of meditation as a way of homecoming – coming home naturally to our deepest and truest self, our self in God in the Spirit.

Whenever I am with a community of meditators I also feel very strongly what a home is. Home is not just a place, but in the deepest sense it is where we are at one with others and where we can be ourselves. Home is where we know others, and where we are known. Home is where we are accepted and accepting. I think that is really the whole meaning of meditation just as it is the whole meaning of the Kingdom of God. It is the whole meaning of our life to know that we really are already at home. John Main often spoke about meditation as the way in which we are first of all restored to ourselves. Through meditation we come back into touch with ourselves so that we can then move out beyond our narrow limitations to others and to God.

During this retreat we will have a real opportunity of grace, to understand the meaning of that dynamism of coming home more deeply. We can also enter into the experience of it more generously because it is only in the experience of anything that we discover its meaning. The most important part of the time that we spend together will therefore be the time we spend in silence. It's well worth taking time away from one's ordinary daily responsibilities in order to be silent. The purpose of what follows is simply to deepen the way we can all be silent and at home in that silence.

During this retreat I would like to explore three aspects of love because love is the very meaning of our life and of our creation. Love is the great healing power of our life as well as the deepest meaning of all our experience. It also becomes more and more clear to us as we follow the way of meditation, that meditation itself is a way of love – nothing more and nothing less than a way of love. In the light of John Main's teaching and in the light of our own experience of meditation over the years, let us see how richly we can be guided on this path of meditation by understanding the dynamic of love as love of self, love of others, and love of God. When we meditate we come into an experience of being *at home* in which we can really feel, perhaps for the first time, that we are at ease with ourselves, at home with ourselves, at one with ourselves. At the outset, then, I would like to reflect upon some of the basic principles of meditation.

Aspects of meditation

Recently, while reading a book on Buddhism in America, I came across a reference to a well known Indian diplomat called Apa Pant, who was a great scholar and intellectual, a diplomat, and also a man of spiritual depth. I met him in Italy in 1975, when he was the Indian ambassador there. I was struck by how rare it was to find a man in public life who had such deep spiritual awareness and practice, meditating faithfully every day. I was surprised to read that when he returned each year to his guru in India, the first question he would always ask his teacher was, 'How can I meditate?' Even after thirty years that was his question. And he said that every time he asked the question he would receive a deeper answer, even if it was the same basic response in the same words.

Meditation, as John Main often taught people, is non-competitive. We are not competing with our previous performance; we are not competing with anybody else. We are not competing with St John of the Cross; we are not competing with the other people in our meditation group. That is something we need often to remind ourselves of because the ego is naturally competitive and naturally divisive. Where there is division there is competition, and we can even be divided within ourselves, as it were, trying to compete with ourselves on our own spiritual path. I think it's important to remember as we enter into the silence of this retreat that we are letting go of this competitive tendency.

Meditation is also non-acquisitive. We are not trying to acquire anything because there is nothing to acquire. The dynamic of meditation is not trying to get anything but to *lose*, to let go. It's in the losing and the letting go that we will find everything that we have, everything that we have been given.

I was taught this recently by two people I met. One was a businessman who had spent five years in prison. He lived in the Philippines under the dictatorship of Ferdinand Marcos, and one morning, while he was sitting in his office, the police came in and said they would like him to come down to their headquarters as they had some questions they would like to ask him. They said he would only be there a couple of hours, so he went. It turned out to be five years! During those five years the worst part was that he didn't know when he would be released or if he ever would be released. (In fact, he eventually escaped.) He had been imprisoned on trumped-up charges. But during those five tragic years he said he discovered things about himself and about God and about his marriage for which he will be always grateful. He said they were the five best years of his life, and that there is nothing that he has now that he would trade for those five years. Four years would have been too short; six years would have been too long. Five years was just right!

What he experienced was a total letting go of his life. He was able to see his family when they came to visit him, but he said the worst part of it was that he was by nature a man always in control. He was always the boss. In his family and in his marriage he was the person who made the decisions and so on. His wife said that she had always been very happy to have him make all the decisions and she could just sit back and criticize. But suddenly they found their roles reversed, and so in a sense they were both in prison during those five years. They both experienced a total letting go of everything that their life had been and a re-forming of their familiar personalities. Their identity wasn't destroyed, but they simply had to let go of it. It was an enforced renunciation. The grace of it and the transformation that took place in him is very similar, in some ways, to the kind of transformation of life that one sometimes hears about in people who have come very close to death.

The other meeting that I had recently was with a woman who had lived in New York for much of her life and had been meditating for about eighteen months. At this time, she left New York because she found the pressure of life was too much to endure. She felt too isolated, too lonely, too alienated, and the stress of the city was too great. She moved out of the city and her life became very complex for a number of reasons, including commute to her work each day. But she said that as she started to meditate she suddenly began to see everything around her differently. All the same relationships, all the same routines that she had been doing before, now took on a completely different meaning; as the months went by she began to discover a new view of life. A new horizon of meaning began to appear before her along with a new flavour to life. She noticed that the old feeling of alienation and isolation began to crumble; it began to dissolve, and instead of feeling isolated and alienated she began to feel in touch. She realized that she had a great network of relationships, both professional and personal, and that they were no longer threatening to her. They were relationships in which she could move out and expand if she chose to, or if she felt called to. Life became no longer a threat or a problem, but more of a mystery, a vocation.

We may not all have had these specific experiences, but we can all go through the same kind of transformation. For all of us, there has to be this radical letting go whether it's enforced by being picked up and thrown into prison for five years and having your life suddenly interrupted dramatically, or in some other way. Maybe it's an illness; maybe it's a new view of life; maybe it's just the phases of one's life unfolding. In some way we have to learn to let go if we are to be able to live freely. We have the great gift in meditation of being able to let go, at our very centre, of all acquisitiveness and competitiveness. What seems like a prison then becomes a school; what seems like alienation shows as relationship.

Learning stillness

Stillness is a wonderful teacher, and we learn this renunciation and this new vision through learning to be still. Being who we are – that's all we have to do. Sometimes, seeing who we are, being who we are, and seeing what is all around us comes as a shock. Sometimes we resist it because our images of ourselves are so strong, and our judgments of other people are so strong, that we won't or can't let them go. We have created a view of the world with ourself in the dual position of judge and jury, and it's very difficult for us to let go of that vision of the world. It involves the shock of conversion, of liberation in some way or other. In the stillness comes knowledge – 'Be still and know that I am God' – and in that knowledge we come not only to know God, of course, but to know ourselves, since we cannot know ourselves without knowing God. And so the stillness of meditation, which is the discipline we practise day by day, is the stillness in which we stop doing, we stop thinking, we stop judging, we stop planning, we stop analysing. But all this stopping is the way to make a new beginning.

As we learn to be in that stillness, a knowledge of the spirit arises, and in that knowledge we find our way forward. One of the great principles of meditation – one of the first things we discover in that stillness – is that we can experience life free from all conceptual reference. In other words, we don't have to think about life in order to live. So often our ideas get in the way and block us from experiencing the fullness of life. In meditation we are very simply letting go of conceptual frameworks in which we try to imprison life and reality. As we become free of this conceptual prison in which we live so much of our lives, we begin to taste the freedom of the kingdom, the glorious liberty of the children of God.

This discovery is so simple that it is impossible to describe. You are able to see something, to be in relationship with something which previously you had fixed ideas about, and now you are able to know directly because you have been able to let go of those ideas, judgments, and prejudices. That is what meditation allows us to do in relation to ourselves, in relation to others, and in relation to God. The wonderful and deeply Christian insight is that this knowledge is love, and it is only in love that we are able to know anything fully. In the stillness of meditation, we no longer want to watch, analyse, and control our experience; we learn to let go of all thoughts, and enter into the experience of being as a whole person. We are not, as John Main said, trying to experience the experience.

What happens during our times of meditation is not so important. This is a difficult truth for us to accept, especially when we are new to the practice of meditation, because we are looking for something to happen. We are investing our valuable time into meditation, so we want to be able to judge from immediate results what's happening. It is only gradually that we learn to let go of that greedy, materialistic approach. We begin to realize that what happens in the meditation period is much less important than what happens in our life as a whole. We have a new view of life, a new vision of life. Above all, we find that it is in our relationships with one another, and in our perception of the priority of love, that the experience really bears fruit.

We have also to remind ourselves of the danger of what John Cassian in the fourth century and John Main today called the 'pernicious peace'. It is the danger that arises when stillness becomes something static. The true stillness of the spirit is a very dynamic and energizing power. This is why when we meditate we feel renewed, refreshed. We find a new energy and a new clarity emerging in our lives, a new depth, a new vitality. But we can easily slip into a false stillness. Even experienced meditators can fall into this danger, which is why it is so important to meditate in a group and community which challenges and stimulates us. Even when we've been on the path for some time it's very easy for us to slip into some form of self-deception or self- indulgence, and the only thing sometimes that can prevent us from slipping off the narrow path of meditation is the critical loving guidance of others with whom we make this journey. Meditation creates community, and we meditate within community.

There is nowhere in the world, however, where I have experienced community that I haven't also found conflict. And yet the act of faith with which we meditate brings us into relationship with others – not a perfect relationship, but a teaching and mutually enriching relationship. A real grace of God is present in such a loving and truthful community, and must be respected and venerated because the help and guidance that we need to reach our destination is to be found in the grace of that community. Both the Christian and Buddhist traditions give enormous value to friendship for anyone on a spiritual path.

Questions for Reflection:

1. 'Through meditation we come back into touch with ourselves so that we can move out beyond our narrow limitations to others and to God.'

What limitations do I perceive in myself which might keep me isolated from others? How can I help overcome those limitations?

2. Silence is the silence of deep communion, not of isolation or withdrawal. What has been my understanding of silence so far? Am I open to other levels of silence?

3. What public figures do I recognize as being marked by a 'deep spiritual awareness and practice'? What makes him/her stand out from the crowd?

4. 'The dynamic of meditation is not trying to get anything but to lose, to let go.'
In what areas of my life can I discern a need to let go?

Application:
'What we learn in meditation, through the utterly simple practice of stillness and of letting go of all thoughts, is that we are able to enter into the experience of being as a whole person and, therefore, the experiences that happen don't matter.'

I will enter my times of meditation without demands or expectations. I will be as simple and generous as I can and give my fullest attention to the sound of the mantra.

> Whatever happens, say the mantra. Say it until you can no longer say it. And as soon as you realize you have stopped saying it, start saying it again. Here is a formula, utterly simple, utterly practical, that can lead any sincere and serious person into the experience-in-itself which is the experience of being, the knowledge of God. As modern people we may find that refreshingly and attractively simple, but we immediately try to find a way around it. One of the easiest ways to avoid the demand of such simplicity is to say in an emphatically moderate and sweetly reasonable tone of voice, 'Well, of course, say the mantra, but don't say it the whole time. Just say it until it leads you to an experience and when you are there relax into it and enjoy the

> experience.' But Christian prayer is about more than relaxation. It is about peace, a state of divinising energy, not just of recharging mental batteries. It is about more than sharpening our self-conscious awareness; it is about knowing the mind of Christ. (Laurence Freeman, *The Selfless Self*, p. 105.)

Meditate for thirty minutes.

Part Two

Distraction

One of the great teachings that the tradition has to give us is simply to stay awake. 'Stay awake and pray,' Jesus said. What John Cassian called the 'pernicious peace' he also called the 'lethal sleep', which is a state that people can remain in for many years or slip into at any time. It is known at time by every meditator. Sometimes the mantra guides us into a state of peace, tranquillity, harmony, and a deep sense of well-being. At that point many people think the mantra is no longer necessary: 'I no longer need to let go because I have been given what I have been looking for. I don't have to let go of this peace because this is the very thing that I've been trying to acquire.'

We have to remember that the poverty of meditation which we accept in our fidelity to the mantra has no limit. So the danger of the 'pernicious peace' is only really overcome by reminding ourselves of the wonderful and absolute quality of poverty which the mantra invites us to and which we freely accept by saying it.

We often feel discouraged because of our distractions. I heard a wonderful description of this the other day by somebody who said that they had been meditating for a while and they were still constantly distracted, but had come to the conclusion that the best approach they could adopt to their distractions was just to be in the presence of them, like an old man watching his grandchildren play. It's a nice image suggesting both comparison and detachment towards one's self. Let the thoughts, images, and fantasies run around if that's what they're going to do, not trying to fight them off, but remaining gently faithful to the work of the mantra, not judging our meditation.

Sometimes, after people have been meditating for years, they feel they've made no progress because when they sit down to meditate they feel their minds are full of the same nonsense, the same problems, the same obsessive thinking and imagining that's been going on from the beginning. Meditation is constantly showing us how much it is a way of life, not just a way of prayer, and that if we are consistently finding ourselves distracted we should look at some aspects of our lifestyle which might encourage this distractedness. This may then call us to reflect upon our lifestyle, to see whether there are activities or practices in our life which we could change or give up which are perhaps the cause of some of our distractedness. 'What you want to be like at the time of prayer,' the Desert Fathers and Mothers used to say, 'you should be like that the whole time.' We have to be able to face those distractions with a sense of detachment, and with detachment comes the essence of prayer which is attention. We learn to pay attention with our whole being: not just 'thinking' with our minds but with our whole being – our body in stillness, our mind and spirit in still fidelity.

Letting go

Meditation connects us with our own mortality. When I was in New York, the husband and the father of two of the people who had been on the retreat there, was dying after a long illness. As I sat with him, knowing that this was a tremendous liberation from many years of great suffering for him and for his family, I realized how much meditation offers a simple acceptance and entry into the mystery of dying. This is nothing less than letting go.

All our life is really a lesson in letting go, and we learn it by stages in different ways. Our whole life is a preparation for this ultimate letting go, this moment of death, in which we are meant to be ready, to be prepared. Anyone who has ever been with someone when they have died will know that that moment has tremendous significance. The whole of our life is focused on that moment. John Main taught that what we are like at the moment of death is of great importance. Our daily meditation is an experience of letting go, of dying to our acquisitiveness, our competitiveness, our prejudices, our self-centredness and egoism; it is a preparation for that moment of total encounter with reality, that moment of total liberation.

Daily meditation teaches us to 'keep death constantly before our eyes'. This is how St Benedict described it to his monks. We might say it is to be able to face the impermanence of life, to face the fact that since things are always passing away, we have no abiding city. The teachings and parables of Jesus also remind us to live in the present moment, not to try to build false securities, false empires; to face impermanence, not with fear, despair or rage, but with confidence and faith, so that in facing it we can discover what is changeless. One of the great gifts that meditation brings to us is to be able to see not only how impermanent and precious *life* is, but also how impermanent *everything in* our life is. Everything is impermanent, even the things we hold most precious. We need to be able to look directly and fearlessly into that impermanence and see what is changeless and what is real in the midst of it. This requires great simplicity, the simplicity that the mantra teaches us. If you are too clever you miss the point. You have to learn to be simple, and the mantra is the great teacher of simplicity.

How can I meditate? I sit down. I sit still and close my eyes. I begin to say my mantra and I repeat my word continually over and over again throughout the time of the meditation. The mantra I recommend is the word *Maranatha*. The word is Aramaic, the language that Jesus spoke. It is a sacred word of our faith tradition. If you choose that word, say it as just four syllables, 'Ma-ra-na-tha'. As you say the word give it your attention. Don't say it with force or violence; don't say it in haste. You're not in a hurry. And don't say it with any desire or expectation. You're saying it in order to let go of everything, not in order to acquire anything. You are saying it in order to come to that poverty of spirit in which we can learn to accept what is being given to us. Meditate twice a day, morning and evening, no matter how you feel, understanding that meditation is a discipline, a learning process.

We must learn to be faithful because in our meditation we are entering into the deepest relationship of our life. We must come to our meditation as if we are approaching the person we love most in the world, and what is needed in all relationships is fidelity. So we enter into meditation with fidelity, knowing that in the discipline of it we are becoming true disciples, true learners. We're not judging our meditation; we're not comparing it. We're allowing it to be integrated into our daily life so that it becomes a normal part of our life. The simplicity of that commitment, that discipline, opens up a path in which everything in our life can be channelled.

On a retreat like this we have an opportunity to re-commit ourselves to that vision and to know with great gratitude that the path is there and that we are on it and that what we're looking for is what we are already doing. We learn that in the seeking there is the finding. During this retreat we also have the opportunity to be more deeply harmonized with the truth of that teaching and with the truth of ourselves.

Life as kairos

Certain moments in life, like the moment of death, are more significant than others. In the New Testament, the word for that significant moment is *kairos*. It's a special moment of time, not just an ordinary moment. I think a retreat like this is for each of us in a unique way, but for all of us in a similar way, such a *kairos* moment – a moment of opportunity, a moment of grace, a moment of deeper transition. And it is an opportunity for us to simplify our life. Most people today are looking at their lives and realizing how complex they have become, and are desperately seeking ways in which they can simplify life. On a retreat like this, we are able to do this.

We come away from our normal environments and put aside our normal routines. We should take full advantage of that, so that we don't bring into the time of retreat too many of the daily anxieties, complexities, and old problems. We will have to go back to those in a couple of days, but during this special time we have the opportunity to simplify our life and, I hope, to come out of this retreat with a sharper understanding of how we can keep our life simple and attuned to the essential values to which we are already committed. This practice of simplicity is the key to a balanced life.

One of the other things we learn in a retreat like this is how to balance our life a little more finely, and how to slow down. We can learn a new respect and a new reverence for the inner harmony that is our true nature. When we are out of harmony, or when we feel stressed, or when we feel we've lost the vision of hope and of love, we are not being true to ourselves. We have fallen out of the truth. But we can always do very simple things to get back into harmony and peace.

The first thing is to slow down a bit. It doesn't mean we stop doing something, but it means that we do it a little more slowly than we're used to. So we should take time to relax. If the weather is good you may be able to spend some time outside walking. Not to get anywhere, just to walk.

In the morning especially spend some quiet time and take perhaps twenty minutes of that time for spiritual reading. During that twenty minutes take as short a piece of Scripture as you possibly can – just a few verses. You might take, for example, a verse like 'Such a hope is no mockery, because God's love has flooded our inmost heart through the Holy Spirit he has given us' (Romans 5:5). Simply read the verse and remain with it, repeating it, reflecting on it, letting it sink into your heart and into your mind. Such reading is very different from the way we read during the week when we want to read as much as possible as quickly as possible to get the information in and to make ourselves more knowledgeable. Forget that way of reading altogether; slow down and read the verse or the few verses that you choose as attentively and as repetitively as you can. The body and the mind need to be exercized, but exercized in a peaceful and relaxed way so that the spirit can be fully opened up. Therefore, the whole of your retreat schedule will focus on your periods of meditation. That is the real work of our lives. But if we can do all things mindfully, carefully, reverently, then we come to that time of meditation more prepared and more open.

St Benedict says, 'God shall be glorified in all things, in everything we do'. There's a wonderful story that parallels that saying. It is a story of the Buddha sitting beside a well. An old woman who comes to draw water from the well comes to him and asks, 'How can I be enlightened?' And he tells her, 'Watch your hands while you are drawing the water.' In other words, we should be present to the mystery of the ordinary which is always there, and to keep that centredness in our attention whatever we are feeling. This kind of mindfulness glorifies God.

At a time of retreat like this when we do stop and slow down, sometimes the feelings that come up are not always peaceful or joyful. Sometimes some of the things we have repressed or haven't given ourselves time to feel will come up. So if you spend some absolutely miserable times during the retreat don't be depressed about it! If we can learn to find this simple place of presence in ourselves, which is the shrine of the Holy Spirit within us, we're able to take whatever comes and to take it in a way which will lead us to a deeper change of heart.

Let us focus on love as the central and unifying mystery of our lives. One of the great sayings of St John is, 'Whoever loves, lives in God' (see 1 John 3:16). He doesn't say 'Whoever loves God lives in God', but 'Whoever loves lives in God'. St Paul expands on this insight when he says,

> With this in mind, then, I kneel in prayer to the Father, from whom every family in heaven and on earth takes its name,

> that out of the treasures of his glory he may grant you strength and power through his Spirit in your inner being, that through faith Christ may dwell in your hearts in love. With deep roots and firm foundations, may you be strong to grasp, with all God's people, what is the breadth and length and height and depth of the love of Christ, and to know it, though it is beyond knowledge. So may you attain to fullness of being, the fullness of God himself. (Ephesians 3:14-19)

Questions for Reflection

1. Are there aspects of my life which contribute to distractions during my times of meditation? What changes can I make to ease those distractions?

2. When I die I will let go of many possessions and many people. How can I be less possessive now?

3. How does meditation lead me to an attitude of non-possessiveness? How can I be non-possessive about the times of meditation?

4. What daily problems and worries can I put aside during this time of retreat so that afterwards I can perhaps return to them with a renewed outlook?

Application:

I will take time each day for periods of spiritual reading. I will let the Word of God enter more deeply into my mind and heart every day. During my meditations I will listen more attentively to the sound of the Word.

> What is so challenging about meditation is the way it leads us to the experience of non-experience. This is what poverty of spirit is about. We always want to know what is happening. We want to know what is going to happen. We want to know what happened. Such desire for knowledge is intrinsically possessive. But if we are truly committed to the pilgrimage of personhood and so truly disciples of the Spirit we are not acquiring experience or seeking enrichment from it. We are entering the experience of non-experience, that poverty of spirit where we enjoy everything by possessing nothing. (Laurence Freeman, *The Selfless Self*, p. 105.)

Meditate for thirty minutes.

Part Three

What is love?

> Dear friends, let us love one another, because love is from God. Everyone who loves is a child of God and knows God, but the unloving know nothing of God. For God is love; and his love was disclosed to us in this, that he sent his only Son into the world to bring us life. The love I speak of is not our love for God but the love he showed to us in sending his Son as the remedy for the defilement of our sins. If God thus loved us, dear friends, we in turn are bound to love one another. Though God has never been seen by any man, God himself dwells in us if we love one another; his love is brought to perfection within us. Here is the proof that we dwell in him and he dwells in us: he has imparted his Spirit to us. (1 John 4:7-13)

Love is the first and the highest gift of the Spirit. In the fruits of the Spirit as St Paul describes them in Galatians 5, love is the first: Love, joy, peace, patience, kindness, goodness, fidelity, gentleness, and self-control. And when St Paul is talking about the gifts of the Spirit, in 1 Corinthians 12, he tells us to pursue the highest gifts, and love is higher than any wonderful extraordinary experience that might befall us. Jesus sums up his whole teaching in one single commandment which he says is a new commandment, 'Love one another'.

Love, according to John Main, is the fruit of meditation. Our progress in meditation is visible in our developing capacity to give and receive love, and to see with our own eyes that love is the central reality of our lives. There is no greater gift, no greater power than this vision of love which is the source of all meaning in our life.

Love is everywhere

One of the great scientific discoveries of modern times was made quite recently. Scientists had been scanning the cosmic skies for years trying to find the source of background radiation of the universe Finally they found this evidence that the universe as we know it came into being in a single act of creation, which they call the 'big bang'. They say that everything that we can possibly know, including time and space, came into being out of this primal unity, exploding out of the concentration of energy into matter. From that moment of creation a radiation energy was emitted that still pervades the entire universe. It bathes the universe. There is nowhere in the universe – no atom, even – that doesn't contain something of that original energy of the act of creation. And it's a most wonderful image of love which, in the deepest understanding of creation, is the origin of creation. God who is love is the creator and God is everywhere.

I met a woman some time ago who, to her own great amazement, is going through a remarkable series of 'revelations' (as I suppose Julian of Norwich might call them) – deep understandings of God and of life. She has come to these understandings with very little religious background, so she speaks with a strong directness and freshness. One of her remarks which gave authenticity to her experiences, was when she said that it seemed to her that before creation, before what the scientists call the 'big bang', there was just love, nothing anywhere but love; and that the best way that love could devise to express itself was to create – to bring creation as we know it into being. It's a very simple idea but it's an idea of startling implications. Love is the deepest vision of which human beings are capable – a deeper vision even than the scientific vision – and if love is the creative source of the universe, then love is everywhere. Love also pervades every human being, every atom, every relationship, every thought, every act.

It is this universal energy of love that unites the inner and outer worlds of our existence, the inner world of our private, solitary selves with the outer world in which we live and relate, create and destroy, love and hate and fear and so on. The same love that is in our own deepest personal core is the love that surrounds us and pervades all external reality, the external dimension of reality. So love is the great uniter, the great unifier. And it is the true nature of consciousness. Love is the great field of unity we are always seeking.

Love, we all know, is the strongest and the most human of our needs. Doctors seem to agree now that if a child lacks affection, tenderness, love, and concern, even the best physical treatment will not allow that child to develop physically or in any other way. Our need for love is deeply embedded in our biological nature. Because it is our deepest and most human need it is also the occasion of our most painful wound, whenever, even unconsciously, we experience an inadequacy of love. And we all know that love decides the quality of our life, although we often act as if we were above our need for love.

Depending on the presence of love in our life we are happy or unhappy, we are free or unfree, we are joyful or we are depressed. If love is flowing in our life, if the inner and the outer dimensions of our life are united by love, then we are fully alive. There's a wonderful description of this in Tolstoy's *Anna Karenina* where one of the characters who is in love goes out in his carriage and as he looks out on the world through the carriage window, everything is bathed in beauty and richness, excitement and vitality. He feels euphoric. Everything is fully alive. Then in the next chapter there's another description of somebody who is depressed and isolated and unloved and unloving, and the world looks completely the reverse. As human beings we see the world either with the eyes of love or with the eyes of a painful absence of love. It's the very simple ingredient that makes or breaks our life.

Forms of love

Our modern idea of love is culturally limited to erotic love. By this I don't mean just sexual love but erotic love in the sense that that phrase was used by the early Christian writers, a love that is centred upon ourselves only. This obsessive, egoistic, desiring love has a tragic dimension: it ends in death or disappointment. It's the kind of love we see in Wagner's opera and in much western literature, the kind of love that is often described in popular songs and soap opera. Erotic love is seen as tragic because it is notoriously impermanent, because it arises and dies in passion. It is individualistic, making us lonely and trapping us in its own impermanence. I think that this modern, culturally bound understanding of love needs to be touched and broadened by a spiritual understanding of love as creative and redemptive, as 'transpersonal'. This does not mean that it is impersonal - you can't have an impersonal love. Love is between persons, uniting persons, but it transcends the individuality of the person experiencing it. It is not limited by the narrow, egoistic individuality of those who are falling in love.

The religious vision of love comes to us, of course, through all spiritual traditions, but especially in the Christian scripture, in St John. 'God is love and whoever lives in love lives in God and God lives in him' (1 John 4:16-17). I think when we meditate we transcend the culture-bound understanding of love as only erotic because we move beyond the limitations of the desires and fears of our ego and break out of the force that leads to tragedy, loneliness, disappointment, and despair. Even when the passion that fuels erotic love fails and dies, we can break out into a new vision of love that is of God, the vision of love we find in the New Testament, the vision of love that enables us incredibly to equate God and love. I think this can only happen through our experience of the impermanence of erotic love.

Seeing the distinction between erotic and spiritual love does not mean the erotic is rejected. It has a great role in helping to attract and deeply bond individuals. It needs to be celebrated in its own season, not repressed. But it does not last for ever. It points to another form of love which does last for ever.

This is why John Main insists so often that meditation is a way of experience. We are experiencing the impermanence of all things, including our most passionate attachments and desires. It is the experience of a love deeper than this impermanent state to which meditation leads us and which renews our spiritual vision. And so to meditate is to become a student of love.

We come to see how deeply love is at the centre of every activity. It is the wavelength of every communication. Love is the background radiation, the background energy of everything we are and everything we do. It is the ultimate meaning of all our experience. We seek love because it is our deepest human need. We also fear it because it can so often lead us to pain, being so closely associated with the loss of our familiar sense of identity. We find that when we love we change. We become a different person or at least a different form of the same person. Because there is death involved in the loss of our fear, desire, and complex defence mechanisms, we often evade what we desire. We long for love yet we run away from it. We set up the circumstances for it to flourish and then we destroy those circumstances. We enter into relationships and then we turn on those relationships. We give and then we take back. We open up and then we contract. So as human beings we discover through love just how complex we are and how self-contradictory we can be. We discover through meditation just how many inner conflicts and inner tensions we have.

One of the things we begin to learn through meditation is that we project on to others and on to relationships the very conflicts that are going on unconsciously inside us as a result of feeling unloved, unwanted, neglected, or abused. We seek and we fear love, and yet love draws us on because love is greater than our own capacity for it. It is all the same love because there is only one love, one creative energy, that is manifested at different levels of reality.

As we grow from infancy to childhood to adulthood to old age, we relate to the world in different ways at each of the stages, but the same love is manifested. Our capacity to receive it and respond to it changes, but the same love is constant. We see the same love in the simplest organism, a single cell. We see it at work in the power of sexual attraction throughout nature. We see love involved in the meeting and the marriage of minds and persons. And we see the same love fulfilled in the union of hearts. We find that our human experience of love develops with our stages of growth. We have to grow up and become adults if we are to realize our capacity for love and be the person we are called to be. Our greatest pain would be to not be the person we are called to be, not growing and developing, not being able to love fully at the stage of life we have reached.

Life is a journey which we pass through by stages, just as in meditation. Understanding that there are stages of development may help us to be patient, rather than trying to impose our own order, our own desire for growth or our own desire for love upon a situation that is not yet ready for it. Patient acceptance of this growth teaches us wisdom. Sometimes, however, these stages are misunderstood and this is where the teaching of John Main on meditation is so important to modern people. It helps us all to see that the journey of life and the journey of meditation are intertwined at every stage and in fact that they are aspects of the single journey of human existence which is simply the journey of love.

Questions for Reflection:

1. 'There is no greater gift, no greater power than this vision of love which is the source of all meaning in our life.'

Do I receive love as freely as I give love? Can I see my life more clearly with eyes of love?

2. To meditate is to become a student of love. Am I a true student or am I a know-it-all? Am I open to the lessons taught by meditation?

3. 'As we grow from infancy to childhood to adulthood to old age; we move to different levels of existence.'
Am I open to growth? Have I been open to growth in the past? Will I commit myself to the process of growth in my relationships?

4. Am I willing to remove obstacles to growth in my relationships as I perceive them today?

Application:
Each day I will open my heart to the possibilities of the life God has given me. I will give myself as generously as I can to the twice-daily times of meditation, recognizing that what may be best for my life is what is most hidden from my conscious mind.

> You repeat the mantra from the beginning to the end of the meditation, or you try to. And trying to, you find that you fail countless times because of silly distractions, recurrent anxieties, daily problems and natural restlessness, because we watch too much television, because we have too many expectations of what should happen. But every time you realize that you have stopped saying the word, very simply, very gently and faithfully come back to it and start saying it again, silently and interiorly The only thing that should discourage you is if you think that you have succeeded! That is a serious problem to solve, to think you are a spiritual success. But persevering in meditation will change all the perspectives of your outlook. Firstly, on meditation itself and next on the values of life as a whole. A discovery awaits, through the experience of depth, of a new way of perceiving yourself and the successes and failures of ordinary life. A deeper meaning, that is of more resonance

> and radiance than anything hitherto suspectcd, begins to be felt. As we persevere we become gradually realised, gradually enlightened, gradually free. We become more loving because the great power released in us as we become simple is the power of love. And so, we say the mantra, not more successfully, but more faithfully. (Laurence Freeman, *The Selfless Self*, p. 102.)

Meditate for thirty minutes.

Part Four

Love of self

Most of us were taught that we had to love God first. Then, having loved God, we must then love other people, and really that was as far as most of us ever went. Perhaps there was a vague mention of loving ourselves because Jesus said that you have to love your neighbour as yourself. But that love of self was usually put last, and also it was usually expressed in negative terms. John Main reversed that order. He said the first step is to love ourselves. The second step is to love others. Then, and only then, can we really enter into the mystery of loving God, or even begin to know what it means to love God. This changing of the order of the stages of our growth in love is of great importance to understanding meditation and persevering in it, because it makes us understand why meditation, which is so simple, can be so challenging. The difficulty is that we are learning as our first step to love ourselves and most of us come to meditation with strong forces of self-hatred, self-distrust, self-rejection.

Most of us, particularly in our religious upbringing, have been taught to be very suspicious of ourselves. When we were taught (at least Catholics) to examine our conscience, even as very young children preparing to go to confession, our first thought was that we must first look for our faults because those are the aspects of ourselves that God is most aware of, and those are the aspects of ourselves that we must be frightened of because we will be punished for them. So we were taught even as young children to consider ourselves as essentially suspect, dangerous, and sinful.

This led, in many cases, to the development of a wholly negative spirituality in which the image of God bore very little relation to the God that we find in the teaching of Jesus, to a God who loves. In this negative spirituality we focus upon our sinfulness, our jealousies, our lust, our greed, our pride, our anger – all the negative emotions or forces in us and all 'mine' – *my* sinfulness. Such egotism can only understand God as a God who rewards, punishes, or condemns. And that is why one of the most dramatic changes that meditation works in our life is a re-visioning of our understanding of God. It is also why many people will say, after they've been meditating for some time, 'You know nothing happens during my meditation. I'm just plodding along day by day, but for the first time in my life I'm able to understand what it means to say that God is love. I begin to understand all this religious stuff about love and all this Christianity. I'm just beginning to see the light through all these years of darkness.'

A negative spirituality, of course, is counterproductive. It tells us that we are essentially sinful. Our deepest identity is that we have a tendency to sin and we must resist it and overcome it. We are full of ego and we must destroy the ego. But a negative spirituality of that kind tends only to distort the ego and reinforce it with new fears, guilts, and shame. Then, of course, our ego is involved in self-contradictory dynamics, conflicts, and tensions within itself, making us feel that we don't understand why we act the way we do. We feel overwhelmed by negative feelings which we call compulsions. We drive the highway of life, veering dangerously from one lane to another.

I think this negative spirituality counts more than anything else for the apparent rejection of institutional religion in the western world today. It explains too why young people, who have been trained in a very different way from the last generation, simply cannot make sense of the institutional church. I got a glimpse into that a few weeks ago when I was reading a copy of *Rolling Stone* magazine. It was the twenty-fifth anniversary issue, a collection of interviews conducted with rock singers over the last twenty-five years, starting with John Lennon and ending up with Madonna. As I read it I was amazed at the subculture I was seeing, and it helped me understand why these were the heroes and role models of the young. They were not exemplary people by any means. They were certainly not saints, but they were honest sinners. It made me understand why these are exactly the kind of people that Jesus hung out with and why it was so shocking to the Pharisees that he hung out with prostitutes and tax-collectors and so on. Their sinfulness, their weakness, their pride and all the rest is wide open, and it is not denied as we deny it in a negative spirituality. Jesus shows us the danger of aquating holiness with respectability.

This is something that we learn as we meditate. We learn to face our dark side; to face our sinfulness, to face all these complex and self-contradictory dynamics going on within us. And we learn to face it without self-deception, without repression, without pious evasion. We face it and accept responsibility for who we are in ourselves. We go beyond the divisions which a negative, self-rejecting spirituality imposes on us.

How we love ourselves

What finally heals the wounds of self-division is love. Love unites, unifies, and heals the wounds of the divided self. It overcomes the deep wounds of our alienation and simplifies us. This is the real meaning of love of self and this is why we have to begin with ourselves.

The Christian contemplative spiritual tradition teaches that our knowledge of God must begin with our knowledge of ourselves. As St Augustine said, we must first of all be restored to ourselves so that we can then become a stepping stone and transcend ourselves and rise to God. I think what meditation teaches us is that we can only love ourselves if we can accept ourselves as we are. We must recognize and see our wholeness, and put the dark side into the picture and accept that dark side as part of it.

In this vision the body and the mind can be seen to be dancing in the spirit – perhaps not dancing very well, but nonetheless dancing the dance of being.

We learn through meditation how deeply integrated these three dimensions of the human person are. The mind and the body, which form a special dual unity, cannot be separated from the spirit. If we try to separate them we create an illusory world. Most of our negative spirituality does precisely that. It tries to divide the body and the mind and the spirit. We learn from meditation that if we can calm down one dimension of our being, then the other dimensions calm down as well. This is why, when we sit to meditate, we sit still. The stillness of our body helps us to come to a stillness of mind which enlarges into the stillness of the spirit.

All of this leads to the question: How do we love ourselves? Well, I think in reaction to this long history of negative morality and self-rejecting spirituality, we have moved today – sometimes in a conflicting way – to another extreme where we are told we have only to be good to ourselves. Look after yourself; be kind to yourself; give yourself a holiday. If you want to do something, do it. This is where love of self often becomes no more than self-indulgence. It may be necessary and good for us to go to this other extreme a bit. Clearly there is a wisdom in that modern, popular psychology of being good to ourselves, but I think the spiritual tradition and the teaching of meditation reminds us that to love ourselves we must find a middle path between self-denial and self-rejection, on the one hand, and self-indulgence and narcissism on the other. Somewhere between self-rejection and self-indulgence we find our true capacity to love ourselves.

Meditation, we know, is a path of moderation. It's very difficult to stay on the narrow path of meditation. It's much easier to follow the tendency to drift off the path either toward self-rejection and self-denial, or toward a very lax self-indulgence. We see this very clearly expressed today in the spiritual movements of our time. Some movements suggest total self-indulgence. Anything goes.

Do what you like. If it feels good do it, if it does, do more of it. On the other hand, particularly in fundamentalism and some of the cults, there is tremendous rigidity, tremendous fear of pleasure, fear of harmony, and tremendous self-denial. I think what we learn through meditation is how to heal the wounds inflicted by these extremes through the power of the Spirit; and as the Spirit is released the spiritual dimension is opened up and we learn the real dynamic of loving ourselves. We learn to live with the law of that dynamic, first of all by accepting ourselves as we are, without judgment, without partiality. We learn to accept ourselves as we are, with all our faults and weaknesses, and then to know ourselves, to come to understand the meaning of what it is we are accepting. Only as we know ourselves can we see beyond ourselves. Only then can we see that we are not limited to this particular egocentric person that we think we are, but that we are greater than that. Then we see that our true centre is not in ourselves but in God. Through self-acceptance, self-knowledge, and self-transcendence, we learn through meditation that this dynamic of a true love of ourselves arises out of the experience of stillness.

We love ourselves by becoming still. The discipline of stillness is the dynamic of transcendence. The more still we are the more we transcend our limitations. Now stillness does not mean stopping. We can understand what stillness means when we see it as part of the process of growth in nature. There is a very important relationship between stillness and growth. Stillness is not incompatible with action. One of the things we begin to feel as we meditate regularly is that those times of meditation, each morning and evening, open up a new centre of awareness deep within us which is not affected by anything we do, however busy or worried we may get, however involved in external activity. If our meditation is regular we shall find a stillness in the midst of all our activity; in fact the activity flows out of the stillness. We discover through meditation the stillness in which we learn to love ourselves; to accept, to know, and to transcend ourselves. The stillness does not contradict action. In fact, it is the very reason for action; it is the energy of action.

Poverty

There is a stillness in all motion. For example, there is a stillness between two movements, even in the movement of the breath. When we breathe in and out, there is an infinitesimally small moment of stillness, a point of stillness between the breaths. There's a stillness between two waves of the sea. There's a stillness between two notes of music. Wherever there is movement, the dance of being, we will find stillness. And stillness means being effortless. When we are still we are not making any effort of the will. In meditation we are not willing ourselves to love God or willing ourselves to love ourselves or willing ourselves to love our neighbour. We are entering into this effortless and totally natural state. The ego, which is always trying to do things full of effort, on its own terms, finds stillness its greatest challenge, because in stillness we stop trying, we stop making these efforts. In stillness we discover a new freedom that lies beyond effort, beyond our egocentric wills. We discover the effortless being of being in harmony with the flow of life. This stillness is a kind of poverty, a letting go of effort and control; a letting go of the fears and desires that dominate our efforts. In this poverty we discover that it is necessary for us to be poor in order to love.

We cannot love without poverty. We cannot even take the first step of loving ourselves without entering into poverty of spirit which allows us to renounce the passions of control and effort, competition and acquisition, and ego in which most of us have become addictively enmeshed. In poverty we accept impermanence. Impermanence terrifies us because it brings us face to face with our mortality. But impermanence can also be seen simply in terms of this rhythm of being and the stillness connecting acts of motion. There is impermanence but there is also connection and continuity. As we learn what the poverty of the mantra has to teach us, we accept our mortality as part of our growth and we learn to practise non-attachment, non-possessiveness, non-acquisitiveness in all our dealings with each other.

We naturally fear poverty, but we learn from experience that poverty leads us to the joy of the kingdom, which is the joy of letting go. In poverty we possess only what is necessary, nothing more, nothing less. But in this poverty we come to face a fear that is deep and real. It is the kind of fear you have when you are standing on the edge of a cliff. People often have this feeling of being on a precipice at certain stages in their journey of meditation, the fear of just being on the edge, having to let go. There may be some kind of physiological, biological reason for the sensation, but the image of being on the edge, being on a precipice, is very common and very powerful, and the ego always resists the final leap. The ego wants to draw back. The ego, which is this little island of consciousness, a dim light which wants to pretend that it is the whole light and which has, of course, its necessary and important role to play, is not dissolved by drugs or by self-denial or by self-indulgence, or by efforts of the will. All of these tend only to reinforce the ego, to distort it, and to lock it more deeply into its fears and desires. The ego can only be dissolved by love, by opening itself to what lies beyond it to the true light of which it is only a dim reflection. We confront the ego in the form of our distractedness during meditation, but as a result of meditation we also become aware of how distracted we are at all other times – in everything we do, we are never content to do one thing at a time.

If poverty means that we possess only what is necessary, stillness means that we only do what is necessary. Stillness is only the necessary action or the necessary movement, and that is why when we meditate we stop unnecessary thinking. When the unnecessary thinking which dominates us is uncontrolled, it leads to phobias, insomnia, fantasies, and paranoia. We cannot learn to be still without learning to love ourselves. We learn through the stillness of meditation to treat our own anger with compassion, our own irritability with compassion, our own judgmentalism with compassion and tolerance and non-violence. We come dimly to understand as we enter into the school of love that this love of self leads to love of others and to love of God and that this is one love. It is ultimately the same reality.

Questions for Reflection:

1. John Main taught that we must love ourselves first, then others, then God. How does that insight compare with our experience growing up?

2. 'I'm just beginning to see the light through all these years of darkness.'
What dark corners of my life have been touched by meditation? Am I ready to welcome the healing light?

3. 'The stillness of our body helps us to come to a stillness of mind which enlarges into the stillness of the spirit.'
Am I as vigilant as I should be about sitting perfectly still while I meditate?

4. 'Somewhere between self-rejection and self-indulgence we find our true capacity to love ourselves.'
In what ways am I too good to myself? In what ways could I treat myself better?

Application:

With the help of the practice of meditation I will become be more aware of my own goodness. I will accept the gifts God has given me and use them in more loving service of others.

> To grow spiritually is to become less self-conscious and more simple. Progress in prayer cannot be measured except

as we perceive a more pervasive spirit of love enter our daily life, as the Christian contemplative experience must bear fruit in the lives of others. The final word on how to pray is St Paul's first word on it – we do not even know how to pray, but the Spirit prays in us beyond all forms of language. Thus the guiding definition of Christian prayer is that we do not pray and that there are no methods of prayer. 'Our' prayer is our entering the prayer of Jesus, his Spirit which is the stream of love flowing between him and the Father.' (Laurence Freeman, *Light Within*, p. 3)

Meditate for thirty minutes.

Part Five

Solitude and love

We cannot love ourselves in isolation. To be isolated is to hate oneself. If we feel isolated, we don't like ourselves: we feel ashamed, we feel deeply self-rejecting, we feel unloving or unloved. There is an inevitable feeling of shame and guilt because we know at some deep level in ourselves that we are not being the person we truly are and are meant to be. We need others, but solitude is necessary if we are to be able to live with others and to love others. Unless we can learn to be by ourselves and in ourselves, we cannot possibly learn to be in a truly loving relationship with others. And that solitude is the first step that we learn as we sit in stillness to meditate.

Solitude means learning to accept our uniqueness. It can be terrifying to realize that we are unique in the universe. We have never happened before and we will never be repeated. But we can only see our uniqueness if we can transcend our ego-bound vision. To see it is to experience an expansion of spirit, which can be quite frightening because it means letting go of what we are clinging to. This letting go into our true uniqueness is the meaning of solitude.

To love ourselves in solitude and poverty means to love God. It means to experience a deep inner gratitude for the mystery of our creation since we emerge out of the unfathomable mystery of God's love. We become aware of the fact that somehow we are born directly out of the love of God. To love ourselves means to live a life of deep gratitude for being and it gives sense to the whole idea of praising God. I don't think we can praise God unless we have learned to love ourselves. On the other hand, to hate ourselves is to hate God. Whatever pious image we may have of God, if we are not capable of loving ourselves we really hate God and we express it indirectly by the way we treat each other. The reality that we face as we learn to love ourselves in stillness can be hard, but seeing it heals us.

We can learn to see reality. Just seeing it and living with it is healing. It brings us to a new kind of spontaneity, the spontaneity of a child who appreciates the freshness of life, the directness of experience. We must recover this spontaneity in order to enter the kingdom. It is the spontaneity of true morality, of doing the right thing naturally, not living our lives by rule books but by living our lives by the only morality, the morality of love. The experience of love of self gives us a renewed capacity to live our lives with less effort. Life becomes less of a struggle, less competitive, less acquisitive, as it opens up for us what we have all glimpsed in some way at some time through love, that our essential nature is joyful. Deep down we are joyful beings. If we can learn to savour the gifts of life and see what life truly is, we will be better equipped to accept its tribulations and its suffering. This is what we learn gently, slowly, day by day, as we meditate.

Meditation brings us to understand the wonder of the ordinary. We become less addicted to seeking extraordinary types of stimulation, excitement, amusement, or distraction. We begin to find in the very ordinary things of daily life that this background radiation of love, the all-present power of God, is everywhere and at all times.

But it can be hard work. There's a nice story about a disciple of the Buddha who was a rather dull disciple who tried hard but could never really understand anything that the Buddha was trying to teach him about the true nature of reality. The Buddha got rather exasperated with this disciple and so one day he gave him a task. He gave the disciple a very heavy bag of barley and he said, 'Run up this hill with this bag of barley.' It was a very steep hill! The disciple, who was dull but very obedient and sincerely wanted to get enlightened, took the bag of barley on his shoulders and ran up the steep mountainside and didn't stop – just as he had been told to do. He arrived at the top of the mountain totally exhausted. He then dropped the bag of barley and in that moment of total letting go he was enlightened; his mind was opened. He came back and the Buddha saw from a distance that he was enlightened. So it's hard work, this learning to be still, this learning to love ourselves. We each of us have our own bag of barley. It's hard work, but it's a work we do in obedience, not out of our own will. It's in obedience to our Master, the Lord Jesus. It's in obedience to the deepest call of our being which is the call to be ourselves. Listen to this from the first letter to the Thessalonians:

> May Our God and Father himself, and our Lord Jesus, bring us direct to you; and may the Lord make your love mount and overflow towards one another and towards all, as our love does towards you. May he make your hearts firm, so that you may stand before our God and Father holy and faultless when our Lord Jesus comes with all those who are his own. (1 Thessalonians 3:11–13)

Love of others

Listen to this from the Gospel of John:

> I give you a new commandment: love one another; as I have loved you, so you are to love one another. If there is this love among you, then all will know that you are my disciples. (John 13:34–5)

I was talking earlier about the necessary first aspect of love which is love of self – coming to a true self-acceptance, a true self-knowledge, and then being able to transcend ourselves. I said that we can talk about this, theologize and psychologize about it, but we need to know how to do it. I think this is where meditation comes in. The great gift of meditation is that it shows us in very real, personal experience that to learn to love ourselves we have only to learn to be still, to come to stillness. As we face this mystery of love we come to face the understanding that love of self is the necessary condition enabling us to obey that commandment of Jesus to love others, to love one another.

We cannot love others until we have laid this foundation of being able to love ourselves – or to put it another way, because it isn't just black and white like that – the degree to which we can love ourselves is the degree to which we can love others. It's very challenging because some psychologists tell us that the ego has most of its defence mechanisms in place by the age of three. Well, by that age we don't have much control over what we do or what we're like, so it's probably at about the age of eighty-three that we begin to get some inkling of exactly what happened to us in those first three years, by which time most of the people we are capable of loving have gone on ahead of us anyway. But we have time and we have to use the time we have to the best possible advantage and this little mechanism of the ego is necessary for this. It's necessary for the first and second stages of learning to love. We need the ego to love ourselves, we need the ego to love others. The ego of course is not a separate person inside us. It is a psychological process of consciousness, a necessary stage in the growth of identity. We particularly need it to love others because we need to be able to see the other as 'other'. We can't make that leap out of our own limited worldview unless we can see the other as being other than us. That's the first thing.

The second step is to see that the other is not separate from us. But we need to have come to that first perception of otherness, and therefore we need the ego for this process of separation. We need the development of the ego, particularly in those first few years, to separate from the womb, to separate from the breast, to separate from mother and father and family and friends, school and church, and so on. We learn to separate and come to stand on our own feet and be able to take the risk of being ourselves. It's painful and traumatic sometimes, but it is necessary.

But the ego, which allows the first stage of separation to take place, then usually becomes a barrier because it locks us into a view of ourselves as permanently separate. As we float in the womb's amniotic fluid we are in a state of undifferentiated union, communion, with the whole universe. There is no separation between me and everything that is. But in order to become fully alive we have to experience a rupture, a break, a separation from that sense of wholeness, that sense of unconscious communion. We have to experience a 'fall', a break in that unconscious communion, if we are to come to fully-conscious communion. Throughout our life we must learn to recognize the dying and the rising involved in all relationships. But the ego naturally does not like the pain involved in this, and doesn't see much beyond pleasure and pain. It doesn't see any ultimate meaning in suffering. The ego eventually comes to recognize a pattern involved in this process of growth and it resists it, and therefore we become stuck, fixated, locked into an ego level of development. The ego then becomes a barrier that we have to transcend, to leave behind. We cannot follow the Master who calls us unless we leave self behind. So the ego is like a boat that takes us across a river to the other shore but then has to be left behind.

The more conscious we become of this process the more conscious we become of the fact that life itself is relationship and that relationships are God's gifts to us. Eileen O'Hea has spoken about relationships as the 'sacred ground' of our life. Understanding that view of human relationships, we can begin to understand what science is telling us about the universe. Everything is in relationship; there is nothing in the universe, nothing in creation that we can say exists alone or in isolation. I suppose in our culture we are relatively open to accepting the idea that life is about relationship. We are very concerned about our inability sometimes to make good relationships. But I think there's a deep flaw in our general understanding of relationships and a good example of it is the way in which we are able to invade the privacy of the sacred ground of a human relationship, to exploit it, to tear it apart, and to destroy the people who are in it.

Public intimacy

We do that every time we read those newspaper articles on the married life of the British royal family for example. It's the most hypocritical exercize of power by the media, but it reflects something very painfully amiss in our modern understanding of relationships. It exposes, I think, the weakness of modern people in making relationships that last or that have depth. We are ready to invade the intimacy of others, perhaps, to compensate for the painful lack of true intimacy in our own lives. It is not only the tabloids that do this, but even the sometimes sophisticated press. The Sunday Times began to serialize a book of gossip about the Princess of Wales. It's done with commercial malevolence and sheer insensitivity to the sacred ground of human relationships. It's a very powerful indictment of how we today in our 'western, Christian culture' really understand the sacredness of love, the sacredness of marriage, the sacredness of a human relationship.

In any case, what we learn as we meditate is that the self, the true self that we are, cannot be isolated and cannot be objectified. We begin to glimpse that the state of wholeness, to which we are aspiring and which is our deepest longing, is a state in which the oppositions and conflicts within ourselves are resolved and where, in a state of wholeness, we are no longer objectifying ourselves or others. A terrible thing that is done in the press, for example in the way it dealt with the royal marriage, is that it totally objectifies human beings for the sake of making money by selling newspapers. We do this, of course, every time we gossip: we are all tabloid newspapers of sorts in our little information systems that we form in our networks. We do that every time we gossip about another person, when we treat others as if they were objects, knowing in our heart of hearts that what we are saying or suggesting cannot be true. We cannot ever truthfully reduce the person to an object.

What we do when we gossip or destroy a relationship by the way we talk about it, is extract a small part of that relationship, a small part of that person, and make it into an object. We deny the mystery of that person or relationship, and that is a desecration. That is why quite rightly in traditional morality it was a grave sin to practise 'calumny or detraction'. But because of our nosiness today we have lost the sense of that sacred mystery. The self cannot be isolated and it cannot be objectified. We cannot isolate or objectify others, and the highest symbol of this pure subjectivity is God.

Questions for Reflection:

1. Solitude is not the same as isolation. How can I be 'alone' and 'with others' at the same time? How can I avoid isolation?

2. 'Deep down we are joyful beings.'
How deep do I have to go to find joy in my life? Why is it not more evident in my life? What obstacles do I put before my experience of joy?

3. When do I experience my self, others, or God as not being 'other', but as being 'separate'?

4. Are there relationships that I desecrate by thoughtless gossip? Why? How can I show more respect for those relationships?

Application:

Each day I will try to be more accepting of other people. I will look for the good in them and not be so quick to see their faults. I will guard my tongue so as not to spread gossip or rumours.

> The starting point for anyone beginning to meditate, with whatever degree of faith, is to accept that we are confused.... We begin to meditate and persevere in the daily

discipline because the deepest human longing, our deepest need and summons is to find peace and clarity.

At work or with the family or in any relationship, a situation becomes clouded. There is a moment to say, 'Let's sit down and try and talk this through, let's try and get to the heart of our problem.' What that means, in fact, when it is human beings involved, is that we must get to the heart of the people concerned. It is not events or life that is confused. It is people who are confused. We are dis-ordered, and so the heart of the problem is always ehe human heart. The great problem is not will they open their hearts, but will we open our hearts, to release the clarifying power of love? (Laurence Freeman, *The Selfless Self*, p. 95-96)

Meditate for thirty minutes.

Part Six

'God'

Everything that our tradition and our teaching tells us of God symbolizes the sacredness of human love and human relationship. God is a community of love. God is not an isolated being, but a community of persons. If God is love, God must be person. Love cannot be impersonal; that's a contradiction in terms. God is not an abstract symbol of something way beyond our ability to experience or understand. But 'God' is a symbol. The word 'God' and everything that word contains for us is a symbol of wholeness and of the fulfilment of the human person in the divinized state. God is a wonderful symbol for us of the sacredness of human relationships, the Trinity, as Father, Son, and Spirit. These are culture-bound terms, but the words we use are less important than understanding the relationships that form this mystery of God: love receiving and giving and transcending itself in ecstasy. Creation is the ecstasy of God, the ecstasy of this communion of love, and human relationships are the essential means of realizing this state of wholeness which is God. Our human relationships are sacraments. In traditional theological language, a sacrament is an effective sign. It's a sign of what is going on inside us. It is the outward sign of an inward reality, but it's also called an effective sign. That means that it actually brings about what is going on. It is not just a photograph like those on identity cards that get you in past the security guards. It's an effective sign, an effective image or symbol. And that is why we cannot love God without loving each other, and we cannot love each other without loving God.

'Whoever loves, knows God.' Love is our true nature and the true direction of our development. It's the direction in which we must always be growing. We may accept all of that – and it may sound inspiring when we reflect upon it – but it presents us with the very real challenge of how it is actually lived. We may believe it, but how do we live it? To what degree do we regard all the relationships of our lives as the sacred ground of God, as the sacraments of God, and as the means we are given of realizing our destiny in God?

Love your friends

So is it really possible to love others? And what does it mean to love others? I think if we're honest we must say that there is a lot of evidence that it is simply impossible to love one another, certainly on any large scale. For example, can we even love those who are closest to us? Just think about the people we are actually sharing life with in family, in community, with our friends or spouses. We know that what often happens in those close life-relationships is that they begin with an experience of tremendous sympathy, recognition, empathy, romance, enthusiastic mutual acceptance – we fall in love. I'm not only talking about marriage. I'm talking about all close relationships, from friendships to people joining religious communities and so on, as well as marriage. Whenever we enter into relationships that bring us close to another person or to a group of other people we usually begin with this initial experience of attraction. We feel, for example, in this first stage that we will never be lonely again. We have found the answer. You see this in religious communities and, of course, you see it in couples in their early stages of falling in love. And then that first stage begins to wear off.

I remember recently talking with an older woman who said that she now has a curious role to play with her grandchildren because they come to her bringing their fiancés to tea; and they talk and they introduce the boy or girl that they are hoping to marry. She said that she loves meeting them but when they leave, as she clears up the tea things she thinks to herself what a terrible gamble they're taking. If only they knew. Six months or a year after they've married they'll suddenly wake up one day and say, 'Who on earth is this person I'm spending my life with?' And that awakening can often lead to times of conflict when we see for the first time the differences between ourselves and those we felt so powerfully attracted to. We begin to enter into power struggles, with our demands and expectations contributing to conflict. Relationships often become very blaming relationships. We blame the other person or the community, or we blame the structures for disappointing us. And when we blame we usually try in some way or other to punish the other for disappointing us. So we find that committing ourselves to love is a great gamble.

We face here also the problem of today's intensely individualistic culture. You only have to travel a few hours by plane to the other side of the world to realize that other cultures are far less individualistic than ours. When they enter into close relationships such as marriage or community, the conflict of the ego that begins in their close relationships seems less intense than with us. Their sense of individual identity is still there, obviously, but it is far less intense and less cultivated by their culture and far less defended than it is with us. We've no real idea how intensely individualistic we have become. We take it for granted.

Wherever human beings come close to each other the ego becomes stronger. The closer we come to each other, the stronger the ego becomes. That is both the opportunity and the battlefield of human relationships, and it presents to us as a culture today with a very profound problem. It presents us with the problem of commitment. How do we stay in a loving relationship, even with those to whom we once felt totally attracted, either in marriage (with a fifty per cent divorce rate), or in religious community (with decreasing numbers of people who want to commit themselves permanently to community). We face profound and deeply unsettling questions about love. What is love? Is it just what Madonna says it is? Is it nothing more than this erotic, tragic, temporary experience of heightened individualism? Is that what it is? How can we discover that it is anything more than that unless we can enter into commitment, unless we can find the meaning of fidelity in love? I think we can only find the answers and find the way through these problems by first accepting that these are the problems we are facing.

Forms of relationship

When I was in the Philippines recently, I witnessed a remarkable attempt to do this in a small community founded by a middle-class woman in her early twenties who went to live in the slums. She lived there on her own to be with the poor and to live a prayerful life among them. As she stood in line every day waiting hour after hour to collect water from the communal pump she would pray, and she gradually found herself surrounded by young children who would come and ask her what she was doing and could they come and pray with her. Eventually a group of young girls about fourteen or fifteen came to join her every day to pray. Over time they left home and formed a community with her.

That was about ten years ago, and now these young women are in their early twenties – wonderful, beautiful people. They're facing serious questions about their community, about their individual lives and vocations. About ten of us meditators who were there attending a conference went to visit them and took part in a little ceremony they had in which they were committing themselves to a five-year period of formation. The word 'formation' in religious life usually means you are going to be made a Sister of this or a Brother of that. But their idea of formation is very different. They have come to realize that not all of those young women will want to be sisters. Some already feel quite certain that they want to raise families, but they are still part of this community.

The practice of meditation has had a profound influence upon them. While we were there, ten of these young women were making their commitment, and since there were ten of us there, we each stood by one of these young women and took part in the ceremony with them. They were committing themselves to underpin the years of formation by learning to meditate. Learning to meditate is the primary focus. Then follow two or three years of study. But the study isn't just going off and studying theology or Scripture in an academic way; their life revolves around Scripture and prayer and worship. In particular, the year of formation is to discover the gifts each person has, whether it is music or art or service to others – whatever it may be – and to develop that gift as fully as possible.

After that period they then have a year of discernment in which they take the time to reflect very seriously upon the next step that they are going to make in their lives. Actually, before that year they take a year of service going out and living and working with the poor, and then after that, the year of discernment. Finally comes the decision of what kind of life to commit themselves to within the community.

I mention this community just because it is an example of the way meditation is making a very powerful contribution to the development of new forms of relationship. We need to be able to commit ourselves to something we can stay with, something which will give us support through the storms of the ego that we go through whenever we come into close relationship. We need some structure for relationships whether it's in marriage or religious vows or whatever, and the traditional structures are very weak today and may not be appropriate to many people. So new forms of those ancient structures need to be developed. It seemed very significant as we took part in that ceremony, that in their vows they were committing themselves to meditation as an essential part of their personal formation and of their shared adventure of life together.

Love your enemies

As we have seen, we have a problem learning to love even those who are closest to us, so how can we possibly love our enemies? To love our enemies is a basic teaching of the gospel and it's one of the ways in which Jesus actually shows us the nature of God. When he tells us in St Matthew's Gospel that we must love our enemies, he relates our relationship with those who have hurt us directly to the nature of God: God who causes his sun to shine on the good and bad alike. God who is unconditional in the way he causes his rain to fall on the just and the unjust alike. God who is kind to the ungrateful and the wicked. So this commandment to love our enemies is a way of teaching us something of the very nature of God.

Most of us have quite a different image of God. We don't think of God as being kind to the wicked; we think of God as punishing the wicked. But that is not what Jesus tells us of God. He tells us that we must become like God, we must love as God loves; we must be perfect as our heavenly Father is perfect. He uses this idea of loving our enemies as the key to understanding how we can become perfect. The Hebrew word for 'perfect' means 'whole'.

I think we have to be honest with ourselves about the degree to which we as Christians reject that teaching of Jesus. We do it as individuals and we often do it as a church. Look at the way we condemn, punish, and sometimes persecute others we disagree with or dislike. The Old Testament image of God was based upon a belief in the moral integrity of revenge. Today we take revenge, but with a divided heart because we secretly know that we're doing wrong. We're doing something wrong because we've been told to love our enemies. But the Old Testament tells us that revenge is the perfectly natural and just thing to do. Somebody hits you, you hit them back. It is the basis of Israeli foreign policy and of every 'Christian' country's foreign policy too, that if you are attacked you retaliate. If somebody hurts you, you hurt them. Eye for an eye, tooth for a tooth.

And there is a kind of justice in that. Deep down we feel that maybe forgiveness of enemies is fine for the great saints or mystics, people who are out on another plane of existence altogether, but in my life when somebody hurts me in some way or other I shall have to get revenge. We don't call it revenge, though; we call it justice. But Jesus definitely says 'No' to this way of thinking. It is just as difficult to love your enemy as it is to love your friend. It's as difficult to love those who hurt you as it is consistently and constantly to love your spouse or those you live with most closely.

Love your strangers

Thirdly, if we find it difficult to love those closest to us and next to impossible to love our enemies, then how on earth can we love humanity as a whole? How can we really be in a state of universal, perfect and compassionate openness to creation? We need to be honest with ourselves here too about how easily we become desensitized to the global sufferings of humanity. There's a term used by the major charities now who co-ordinate their advertising campaigns in such a way so as not to create 'compassionate overexposure' or 'compassionate burn-out'. If you show too many images of suffering or you appeal to people's compassion too often, in a limited period of time they simply turn off, and there's a skill in learning how to advertise the sufferings of others in order to evoke people's compassion. In that kind of world the whole notion of universal compassion becomes a very difficult one for us to understand.

How can we remain genuinely, sensitively open to the sufferings of strangers, people on the other side of the world, and even to the person sleeping in the shop doorway? How can we really remain compassionate when we're so often embarrassed by them? When we go out to a meal with a friend and we pass someone begging on the street or rolling themselves up in newspapers in the shopfront, we turn away. It embarrasses us, it intrudes upon us. If we see too many images of grief and suffering on the television, we unconsciously turn off and we wait for the next commercial to come on to relieve the insistent pressure of that image.

So, it doesn't look very hopeful so far that we're going to be able to love one another. And yet we come back to the fact that our relationships are the most important things in our lives. Relationships affirm our lovableness and our worth, our dignity, our value, even though the same relationships also trigger off feelings of guilt and worthlessness and often evoke the dark side of us, showing us our capacity for cruelty, revenge, and insensitive behaviour to the weak and socially worthless.

Questions for Reflection:

1. 'To what degree do we regard all the relationships of our lives as the sacred ground of God, as the sacraments of God, and as the means we are given of realizing our destiny in God?'

2. In which of my relationships do I find both love and conflict? How can I keep those feelings in balance?

3. 'Love your enemies.'
For me, is this a realistic or an idealistic goal?

4. What do I consider to be essential in my life? What is not essential?

Application:

I will look to my enemies to learn more about myself. I will try to be more discerning about what is of positive value in my own life. What things that are trivial can I do without? What things have I overlooked that might be of more benefit to me and to those I love? I will do my best to build up those positive aspects of my daily life.

The mantra clears a way through all the thoughts of past and future to reveal, in a thought-free state, the radiant reality of the here and now: the moment of Christ.

It is only in the present moment that we can find God; the God who calls himself 'I AM'.

Living in the present moment is an art that is practiced in daily life. Ordinary life is the best school of meditation for this reason. It teaches the error of identifying God with religion, temple, synagogue, mosque or church, with pious language or with ritual. God is everywhere at all times. Meditation is the daily discipline that teaches us to see God in the here and now.

The contemplative experience is simply being fully conscious in the present moment. We do not have to master any difficult technique or theories in order to meditate. We have only to be at home and to wake up. This is what the mantra helps us to do. (Laurence Freeman, *Christian Meditation – Your Daily Practice*, pp. 25-26)

Meditate for thirty minutes.

Part Seven

How to love others

How do we love those closest to us, then? I think the first way is to learn to see the relationship, the close intimate relationship, as a kind of a ground on which we stand with the other. We stand together in that relationship. In other words, it isn't my relationship, it is the relationship that unites us. We stand as equal sharers in the mystery of that sacred ground. Very often we didn't choose the closest relationships in our lives. Very often we can see people or communities that come into our lives as the sacred gift of God. They are the manifestation of the nature of God through human relationship. So we need to be able to see our relationships with those closest to us no longer from an egocentric point of view (this is my relationship, this is my wife, my husband, my friend, my brother or sister) but from a place where we can say the relationship enfolds us all. The first step in learning to love those closest to us is to realize that the relationship does not belong to me or to anyone within it, but is the ground in which we are all growing beyond our own egos.

The way we learn to love ourselves is to be still, and the way we learn to love others is to withdraw our projections from them. These projections may be positive: 'This person is the most wonderful person I've ever met in the world.' 'This is the most wonderful community I've ever entered in my life. It's got all the answers for me.' 'This relationship is going to fulfil me and satisfy me; it answers every need I have and it will heal every wound I've ever had.' Such idealistic projections have to be withdrawn. To love others we cannot condemn them to play out the roles of our idealized projections. Withdrawing those projections is a major step of maturity and is the work that we perform in meditation.

As we enter into the solitude of our own uniqueness we naturally withdraw those parts of ourselves that we project through fantasy on to others. That's why our relationships change as we meditate day by day. But if we don't withdraw those projections then the 'love' that we initially feel for those who become our idols or ideals inevitably turns to hatred or to conflict. Sometimes you stay in relationship with those people and you continue to live with them anyway. But we all know of marriages where people have stayed together fighting for thirty years, battling because they have disappointed each other in their initial expectations. We also know of many marriages, many relationships, many people in communities, who have worked through those painful, early stages of learning to love one another. They have withdrawn those projections and have learned to allow the other person to be who they are with all their faults and imperfections. They have learned to accept that person as they are and to know them as they are, and then really been able to revere them and to love them. It is only when we can learn to accept others as they are – in their imperfection, in their sinfulness, in their weakness, in their infidelity – that we can really understand them as a sacrament of God and understand our relationship with them as a means of realizing our union with God.

So, in loving those closest to us we have to withdraw our positive projections, the way we idealize people unrealistically. But in learning to love our enemies we have to learn to withdraw our negative projections, the ways in which we 'dump on' others all our own anger, all our own hurt, our woundedness, our own faults. We can all probably point to times in our lives when we have criticized others for the very faults that we ourselves have but did not recognize or accept in ourselves. We usually see this trait more clearly in others than we do in ourselves.

Learning to forgive involves this difficult, complex, and quite painful process of withdrawing our projections from others. Nothing is easier, or gives greater satisfaction, than to blame others for what has gone wrong in our own life. This is the beginning of racist persecutions, ethnic cleansings, and holocausts. This is the beginning of witch-hunts and all kinds of personal or collective inhumanity. This is one of the terrible parts of human nature; that we can take a perverse pleasure in blaming others for their faults, projecting our own problems on to them, making them scapegoats. It happens over and over again in the course of history and in our personal lives. It is the darker side of human nature. But deep prayer allows us to forgive. We learn that the only way is the way of forgiveness. In fact, Jesus makes that the axis of his moral teaching. That is all he tells us to do: love one another. It specifically includes loving our enemies. If we can learn to do that we learn to go beyond the ego, beyond our fear, beyond our self-hatred and beyond our guilt by withdrawing our projection of these forces on to others.

Forgiveness and compassion

We come to realize through meditation that no one can take away from us what is ours. Our own goodness, our own identity, cannot be taken away. That is why we have to understand forgiveness as a process that takes us deep into our own wounded humanity, where we find our true self. Forgiveness can only be complete when it is as complete as the love of Jesus for his enemies; and that can only come about when we know ourselves as fully as he knew himself, and loved himself.

The same applies to the way we love humanity. Just as, in learning to love those closest to us, we withdraw our positive projections and fantasies, so in learning to love those who are our enemies we withdraw our negative projections. Finally, in learning to love everyone we have to withdraw our abstractions. We have to withdraw our statistical mind which is often the way we treat the suffering of others. We do this on a global level when we talk about how many hundreds of thousands of people with AIDS are going to die. We think about the suffering in terms of huge statistics. We sometimes do it in terms of social work, education, or working in hospitals where we undergo training that teaches us to treat the patient or the case as if they were part of a textbook study. Learning to love humanity means being able to treat every member of humanity as a unique individual.

It is here that we come to the great difference between compassion and pity. Pity is when we love someone who is suffering but when the love is still embedded in our own fear. When we see the suffering of another, when we see somebody dying for example, we cannot help but fear our own death; and if we are controlled by that fear, even unconsciously, we pity the person who is dying. 'Poor thing,' we say. ('Thank God it's not me,' we think.) But when our love meets the suffering of the other person and breaks through this egocentric fear in ourselves, we no longer think of the other suffering person as a 'poor thing'; we think of them as ourselves. They are not separate from us. The meaning of compassion is that we recognize that we mourn with those who mourn, we die with those who die, we suffer with those who suffer. This is the compassion of Christ which has united all humanity in himself. 'When you gave a glass of water to the thirsty, you gave it to me.... What you did to the least of my little ones you did it to me.' (Cf. Matthew 10:42; 25:40.)

The only way to cope with the complexity of human relationships is to learn simply to love. We learn that love is the unifying force in every human relationship whether it is a relationship with those closest to us, or those who have hurt us and who may be unrepentant about the way they hurt us, or the way we relate to humanity at large, to the down-and-out in the street or to the suffering we see on our television screens. We learn that it is the same love that relates us to all of those. The only way to deal with the complexity of human relations is the simplicity of love. In love we do not judge, we do not compete; we accept, we revere, and we learn compassion. In learning to love others we release the inner joy of being that radiates outwards through us, touching others through our relationships. This is why communities, families, and marriages do not exist solely for the perfection of the people in those immediate relationships. They exist also to radiate the love of the family, the love of the parents, the love of the members of the community beyond themselves, radiating that joy, that simplicity of love beyond themselves, to touch all those who come into contact with it.

It was John Main's vision of human community, that community is made possible by the commitment we each make in solitude to the most profound relationship of our lives which is our relationship with God. This is why in learning to love others we come to a new insight into the unity of creation and into the basic simplicity of life. We see what it means to say that love covers a multitude of sins. Forgiveness is the most revolutionary and transforming power of which we are capable. It teaches us that love is the essential dynamic of every relationship, the most intimate, the most antagonistic as well as the most casual. It's the very ordinariness of our daily meditation that reveals to us how universal is the way of love.

Love one another

Listen to this from the first letter of John:

> How great is the love that the Father has shown to us! We were called God's children, and such we are; and the reason why the godless world does not recognize us is that it has not known him. Here and now, dear friends, we are God's children; what we shall be has not yet been disclosed, but we know that when it is disclosed we shall be like him, because we shall see him as he is. Everyone who has this hope before him purifies himself, as Christ is pure.... My children, love must not be a matter of words or talk; it must be genuine, and show itself in action.... Dear

friends, let us love one another, because love is from God.'
(1 John 3:1–3, 18; 4:7)

Well, I don't know if you've had enough of love by now. But St Augustine says that loving is the only thing you can't do too much of, so I would like to turn now to the third aspect of love in the scheme I have been using, which is the love of God.

It's very interesting how our deepest beliefs and most personal feelings affect everything we do. I'll give you an example. Some researchers did a project on the judicial system recently. They wanted to see what kind of relationship existed between the way judges performed in court and their most personal, intimate beliefs. The researchers took a group of judges and divided them into two groups. They gave a questionnaire to one group and interviewed them about their feelings about death, asking them when and how they imagined they might die. They asked them questions about who had died of those close to them, and so on. The whole interview revolved around their deepest personal feelings and experiences of death and dying. To the other group of judges they asked less personal, less challenging, less disturbing questions about their general beliefs and background. It was remarkable, apparently, how the judges who had had this fear of death awakened in them were much harsher in the way they passed down sentence that day. The reason given was that our fear of death, the way we deal with the fear of death, is very closely associated with the way in which we shape the world in our own mind. In other words, it affects our conventions, our conventional beliefs, our morality. It affects the way we think the world ought to be, what we think is right and wrong. This moral and social orthodoxy is one of the ways, it seems, by which we defend ourselves against the chaos of death. And so when this fear of death is awakened inside us, when the repression is lifted a little bit and we face death, we react by becoming much harsher, much more violent in the way we defend the conventions of our life, because it is these conventions which make life safer for us.

Whether that explanation is true or not I do not know, but it is certainly an example of the way our deepest beliefs can affect the smallest things we do as well as the most important decisions of our life. How much more important, if that is the case, must our idea and belief of God be. What we believe and feel about God must colour our whole personality, our responses and our relationships. I think you can see this, for example, in the way a fundamentalist believer often reacts in such anger when his belief in God, his idea or image of God, is challenged. What we are doing is shaking the very foundations of the way he sees and lives in the world. We all do it. We see it in all forms of prejudice. We see it in all forms of intolerance. So the way we experience the love of God shapes the way we love ourselves and the way we love others.

There is also a very close relationship between the way we imagine God and the way we experience God. Part of the problem we face when we come to meditation is that there is often a big gap between what we think about God – God in our minds – and what we experience of God – the God in our hearts. This gap between image and experience is one of the wounds within ourselves that is healed by meditation. It is a wound, or division, that for most of us begins in childhood.

Experience and image

Most people can probably remember an experience of God in their early childhood, a direct and complete experience. It may be an experience of overwhelming love, an experience of uncontainable joy or an experience very often for children of profound oneness with everything around them. Perhaps in nature, just looking at a tree, the feeling of being swept up into the unity of creation. Now a child can have that experience very profoundly, but without being able to describe that experience. What happens is that the images, the concepts of God with which the child's religious development is shaped in family, church, or school, often bear no relation to the experience that she has had, and very often even if she talks about that experience or shares it, it is not in relation to 'God'.

Much more often, our image of God is related not to those experiences of love or joy or union, but to experiences of authority and punishment. Young children very often are taught to think of God as a sort of super-parent. The very words we use about God – 'Father', for example – carry with them in most children's upbringing an image of the person in the family who does the correction, the physically stronger parent who does the discipline. The idea of God as Father carries with it, therefore, this sense of control, or dominance. And where there is punishment associated with this kind of relationship to authority there is fear. We fear being punished by daddy or mummy; we fear being sent to hell.

So there is for most of us a deep inner disruption between the powerful image of God in our minds, and the actual experience of God which we may have had as children, which we may still have even now. Through meditation we learn to let go of all the images of God which have formed in us over the years and in letting go of all the images, all the imagining, all the concepts of God that are formed in us, we recover our child's capacity to experience God fully. We regain the child in us whose experience is not controlled by its concepts. That is why Jesus says that in order to enter the kingdom, which is the direct experience of God, we must become like a little child.

Through meditation we learn that the only image of God which is adequate is ourselves. We are the image of God and this image of God is made magnificently visible in Jesus. Jesus reflects to us who we truly are. He is the mirror, as it were, of our true self as well as the image of the invisible God as St Paul describes him.

Meditation is constantly teaching us that we must let go of the God of our minds, our concepts, in order to love God. This is a lesson we learn through all human relationships. To love, we must let go: we must move beyond the image of the other person that may have formed itself in our minds in order to find the reality and on to which we can project positive or negative feelings. A relationship can only be deep and enduring if we are moving beyond the image to the reality. We love only if we are letting go of the person we love. Paradoxically, we cannot be united without this experience of renunciation. The great teaching of the whole Christian tradition is that we can only know God by love. God cannot be contained in any thought or in any mental or legal system or in any place, ritual, or external form. But God can be known by love and therefore we have got to learn how to love God by letting God go.

Questions for Reflection:

1. Who are the ones I love as I stand on the ground of our relationships? How do I share that ground?

2. What 'projections' can I recognize in my relationships? Am I willing to withdraw those projections? What remains then?

3. In what communities, families, and marriages do I witness an outpouring of love?

4. Am I willing to become a 'little child'? What adjustments must I make in my life to allow that transformation to happen?

Application:

I will do my best to develop a spirit of simplicity and acceptance. I will be more tolerant of others, accepting them as part of God's plan for me. I will affirm those around me and be available to them when they are in need.

> We meditate as Christians in the faith that the Word dwells within us, in our heart of hearts. We nourish that faith at other times and in the other dimensions of Christian life with the reading of Scripture and the celebration of the sacraments,

which themselves reveal the same Word that lives in our communities of faith, in our deeper selves and in our minds. So, as we grow in faith, we grow through meeting the Word into a unity of mind and heart, into being a unified person and into a single consciousness. As we grow, the innerness and the outerness of the Word are both necessary for us. A fully developed Christian consciousness unites inner and outer dimensions of consciousness. But when we experience the Word fully, which means when we listen to it totally, just as when we say the mantra with complete and undivided attention, there is effectively no inner or outer. These are merely terms of convenience, terms that we have to use within the limitations of our daily levels of consciousness. But when we are fully obedient to the Word, we encounter the Word in its dimension of utter transcendence. We are one with the Word when we know that we are beyond inner and outer. We are simply one, and reality is then seen as one with us, one with reality. (Laurence Freeman, *The Selfless Self*, p. 115)

Meditate for thirty minutes.

Part Eight

Love of God

I remember some time ago being with a woman who was dying. She was tormented by the fear that she did not love God. She was a good woman; she had lived a good life. But she was facing this tremendous anguish on her death bed and it was only very slowly and painfully that she came to understand that the very desire to love God is itself the love of God. To want to love is to love, but the full flowering of love takes time. The full flowering of love involves an exchange of identity, a laying down of our life and a discovery of ourselves in the other. We find ourselves no longer in the isolated state of our ego- consciousness; we find ourselves now in relationship, existing in the other, with others. The full flowering of love demands reciprocity, a mutual sharing, giving and receiving.

When we use the word 'love' we always have to remember that it means two things united in the same act. It means both loving and being loved. It is not fully love until the loving and the being loved have been balanced. Love is only fulfilled when the passive and the active dimensions are balanced. The receptive, interior, or feminine part of ourselves must be balanced by the giving, outgoing, or male part of ourselves. And God is the balance of love, the 'union of opposites'.

The image of the Trinity is the most profound symbol of the Christian life. It shows us the dynamic balance of love: the giving of love, the receiving of love and the ecstasy of love in the Spirit. Ecstasy is the transcendence of duality. We see it expressed perfectly in the language of Jesus in St. John's Gospel as he describes his relationship with the Father. He does not exclude from his human relationship with his Father all his human relationships with his family, his friends, his disciples and indeed all humanity. He prayed that all might be one as he and his Father are one.

Learning to love ourselves – which is the first step in our entry into this balance of love – requires simply that we learn to be still, that we learn to accept ourselves, to know ourselves, and to allow ourselves to be led beyond ourselves through stillness.

Learning to love others means that in stillness we allow ourselves to accept others and see others for what they really are, not putting them into the moulds of our own emotions or desires. Instead of projecting our own feelings or images on to them, we allow ourselves to relate to them as they are in themselves. Then we are able to see each relationship as something that we share equally with others, as the sacrament of God's love bringing each and all of us to the wholeness that allows us to 'share in the very being of God', as St Peter says (2 Pet. 1:4).

It is love that divinizes us and we learn to love both ourselves and others by entering into the mystery of relationship. Learning to love ourselves goes hand in hand with learning to love others, and teaches us how to love God. It is only by loving that we discover who God is. 'Everyone who loves is a child of God and knows God, but the unloving know nothing of God' (1 Jn 4:8). However many wonderful ideas they may have about God, they know nothing about God if they are unloving, for God is love.

Meditation constantly asks us how we see God. It asks us the condition of this deepest relationship of our life. Jesus says,

> You have learned that they were told, 'Love your neighbour, hate your enemy.' But what I tell you is this: love your enemies and pray for your persecutors; only so can you be children of your heavenly Father, who makes his sun rise on good and bad alike, and sends the rain on the honest and the dishonest. If you love only those who love you, what

> reward can you expect? Surely the tax-gatherers do as much as that. And if you greet only your brothers or sisters, what is extraordinary about that? Even the heathen do as much. There must be no limit to your goodness, as your heavenly Father's goodness knows no bounds. (Matt. 5:43–8)

That is a supreme description of the wholeness ('goodness' or 'perfection') that we all seek – the balance, the integration, the reconciliation of all things in our life in love.

Just as we learn to love ourselves by being still, and learn to love others by ceasing to project our emotions on to them, so we learn to love God simply by allowing ourselves to be loved. Our love of God originates in God's love for us.

> The love I speak of is not our love for God, but the love he showed us in sending his Son as the remedy for the defilement of our sins.... We love because he loved us first. (1 Jn 4:10, 19)

Nothing is more obvious than that God must have loved us first. He has created us out of love for us, but we constantly forget this. What we learn in meditation is to remember: to remember that God loved us first, and as we open ourselves to that truth we experience the love of God flooding our inmost heart through the Holy Spirit which he has given us. We experience ourselves loved, we accept ourselves as loved, we allow ourselves to be loved. That is what we are doing in meditation and, as a direct result of that, we are empowered to love ourselves and love others and love God.

Fruits of meditation

The great resistance to that process is the ego. The ego wants to love God first and, of course, the ego is constantly trying to put itself first. But gradually we learn to move beyond the attempt to love God before God loves us, or even perhaps trying to love God so that he will love us, beyond all the complex ways in which the ego tries to manipulate and control even God through its image of God. In meditation we are still and withdraw our projections.

As we learn to re-centre ourselves in the reality that God loved us first, then the experience of being loved, which is the whole meaning of redemption, impels a response in us. We do not even have to *try* to love others. It is impossible to force yourself to love someone, or to force yourself to love yourself. It is not an act of the will. We are impelled by the very nature of the experience of being loved to become loving. It reveals to us our true nature and our true potential.

But we must not limit the experience of God's love for us just to the emotions, or even to the mind. This experience of the love of God flooding the heart is deeper than the mind and prior to the emotions. It opens us up to the fundamental relationship of our being, the deepest identity we have. It is in this relationship with God that every other relationship, including even our relationship with ourself, is rooted. 'What can be deeper than our relationship with ourselves?' we wonder. What is deeper is our relationship with God, the source of our being. This experience of being loved by God floods the mind and floods the emotions and even floods the body. It transfigures every aspect of our being – our body and all the levels of our mind. It is deeper than all of that, though it can be seen by the mind to some degree and can be felt in the emotions, which are reconciled to our bodies when we become whole. The more we become whole, the more we realize that this love of God is not only the background radiation of the universe, it is what we as whole persons are bathed in.

I think here we discover one of the great fruits of meditation. This experience develops and flowers in us silently and unselfconsciously day by day through our journey of meditation. It sends us back to the words and images of sacred Scripture, not only our own but all Scriptures. It changes our idea of God as it changes our idea of ourselves. We notice words, phrases, and images in Scripture that we did not notice before. For example, we notice that Jesus calls God 'the one who truly is'. We notice that St Paul calls God 'the source, the goal and the guide of all that is'. We begin to understand what St John means when he says that 'God is greater than our conscience' – a very liberating idea which we can only even begin to understand from our own experience of God.

That God is greater than our conscience means that God is deeper than our own self-rejection, deeper than our guilt, deeper than our fear of punishment. It means that God, as St John says, knows all. And we learn this through a combination of our own experience and the teaching of the wisdom-tradition of the enlightened minds of the past. In this way we learn that the only morality is the morality of love. We learn that forgiveness and compassion are not signs of weakness or compromise or condescension, but are the very structure of reality. This is the God who is equally loving to good and bad alike.

Love is from God, St John says. Everyone who loves is a child of God. This experience of loving God is rooted in our capacity to be loved and that is the great quality of the child. A child wants to be loved. It's the most natural thing and is perhaps the only thing a child wants with its whole being: to be loved. It is that childlike capacity to be loved that we recover through meditation, our deepest and truest identity as a child of God. It is this knowledge that we are children of God, wanting to be loved and accepting the poverty of needing to be loved, that heals us. It is that self-knowledge that heals us and heals the whole person, including the psychological reality that we have as a child of our parents, as husband or wife, brother or sister, or whatever. This psychological reality that we spend most of our time thinking about and struggling with is a real part of us, but it is not the whole person. There is a basic distinction between the path of the spirit and the path of psychology. Our deepest identity is our identity as a child of God and it is by discovering that and knowing that, that we release from within ourselves cosmic powers of healing and renewal.

St John says that God has never been seen. In other words, God can never be an object outside ourselves. It is the mind that is always creating objects, always creating an external reality. We do this continually; and because we do so we need, in our prayer, to go deeper than the mind. We need to go to that level of our being, the heart, the spirit, where there is nothing outside us, where we understand that we are in relationship, in communion, in the dance of being, with everything that is, in God. Each of us is called to this and is capable of it. That is why in our meditation we surrender all ideas or images of God as being an object that can be seen or a thing that can be thought, some 'thing' outside ourselves. God has never been seen but dwells in us as we love one another. That is the whole structure of Christian life. God cannot be seen but expands in us if we love one another. And then, as St John says, love is brought to perfection.

Love is one

These stages or aspects of love that we have been reflecting on show us that love is a school. We are learning to love by loving, and meditation is the principal lesson by which we are learning. We learn from it that love is the thing on which we will be assessed at the end of the course. And we can probably already guess that when we come to review our own life, as people do when they know they are dying, the values by which they judge themselves are the values of love, the values of their relationships. The only thing that people want to do before they die is, as far as possible, to put their relationships in good order, to make sure that they take that final step of transcendence with as much free-flowing energy of love in them as is humanly possible for them.

In the light of the experience of meditation we are able to see the balance of love in our life, the great balancing power of love that creates us, that accompanies us throughout our life, that heals and teaches us. We see the love that is with us, that accompanies us on the journey. It is not a love we need to gain or to earn but a love that is constantly with us. Our eyes are opened through meditation to see how much this power of love is present in the midst of all our imbalance, all our own waywardness, all our own distractedness. Even in the distractedness of our meditation we are able to feel more and more deeply the presence of peace. And as it teaches us to love ourselves, to love others, and to love God, meditation also teaches us that all relationships are really aspects of one relationship.

Let us close with listening to these words of St John:

> God is love; he who dwells in love is dwelling in God, and God in him. This is for us the perfection of love, to have confidence on the day of judgment, and this we can have, because even in this world we are as he is. There is no room for fear in love; perfect love banishes fear. Fear brings with it the pains of judgment, and anyone who is afraid has not attained to love in its perfection. We love because he loved us first. (1 John 4:16-19)

Questions for Reflection:

1. When I look at my relationships with others can I find the dual aspects of *loving* and *being loved*? Can I find those same aspects in my acceptance of myself?

2. 'Learning to love ourselves and learning to love others goes hand-in-hand, and teaches us how to love God. It teaches us who God is since it is only by loving that we discover who God is.' What can I learn about God through my every-day relationships? Who brings me God in my daily activities? How has my awareness of God changed because of my relationships?

3. 'God loves us first.'
How does meditation nurture this insight? Do I find God at the root of all my relationships?

4. 'Meditation sends us back to the words and images of sacred Scripture, not only our own Scripture but indeed all Scriptures, and it changes our idea of God as it changes our idea of ourselves.' When I listen to the word of God in Scripture, do I attend to the words and hear them as if for the first time? Do I respond to the Word with an open heart?

Application:
I will accept myself as a child of God. I will read the sacred Scriptures every day and listen not only with my mind but with my heart. I will nurture in myself child-like qualitites of gratitude, wonder, joy and curiosity. I will be more ready to recognize those qualities in others, and look for opportunities to accept them and nurture them. To reach this sensitivity, I will resolve to be as faithful as I can to my twice-daily periods of meditation.

> So, by our conversion we arrive at mindfulness of the one Christ present in our hearts and in the world, not remembering Jesus by turning our imagination to the past ('We no longer know Christ after the flesh' [2 Cor. 5:16]) but mindful of his presence in the present moment. And it is the mantra that anchors us in the present moment. This mindfulness is Christian enlightenment: illumination by the mind of Christ, by his consciousness which has been transfigured into pure love, by the light of divine love. We awaken to this presence at the deepest level of consciousness. It takes time for it to break the surface of our consciousness but as it rises to the surface, as the light begins to spread through our consciousness, so the depth of our mindfulness grows. And that is our entry into the all-pervading consciousness of the risen Christ. (Laurence Freeman, *Light Within*, p. 19)

Meditate for thirty minutes.

The World Community for Christian Meditation

Meditation in the tradition of the early Christian monks and as John Main passed it on has led to the formation of a world-wide community of meditators in over ninety countries. Weekly groups meet in many kinds of places and number over a thousand. An International Directory is maintained at the Community's London International Centre. A Guiding Board oversees the direction of the Community, a quarterly newsletter, the annual John Main Seminar, the School for Teachers, and the co-ordination of the Christian Meditation Centres around the world.

Medio Media

Founded in 1991, Medio Media is the publishing arm of the World Community for Christian Meditation. It is committed to the distribution of the works of John Main and many other writers in the field of contemplative spirituality and interfaith dialogue. Medio Media works in close association with the British publisher Arthur James. For a catalogue of books, audios, and videos contact Medio Media Ltd at the International Centre in London.

Christian Meditation Centres

International Centre

International Centre
The World Community for Christian Meditation
23 Kensington Square
London W8 5HN
Tel: 0171 937 4679
Fax: 0171 937 6790
e-mail: 106636.1512@compuserve.com

Australia

Christian Meditation Network
P.O. Box 6630
St Kilda Road
Melbourne, Vic. 3004
Tel: 03 989 4824
Fax: 03 525 4917

Christian Meditation Network
B.O. Box 323
Tuart Hill, WA 6060
Tel/Fax: 9 444 5810

Belgium

Christelijk Meditatie Centrum
Beiaardlaan 1
1850 Grimbergen
Tel: 02 269 5071

Brazil

Crista Meditacao Comunidade
CP 33266
CEP 22442-970
Rio de Janeiro RJ
Fax: 21 322 4171

Canada

Meditatio
P.O. Box 5523, Station NDG
Montreal, Quebec H4A 3P9
Tel: 514 766 0475
Fax: 514 937 8178

Centre de Méditation Chrétienne
Cap-Vie
367 Boulevard Ste-Rose
Tel: 514 625 0133

John Main Centre
470 Laurier Avenue, Apt 708
Ottawa, Ontario K1R 7W9
Tel: 613 236 9437
Fax: 613 236 2821

Christian Meditation Centre
10 Maple Street
Dartmouth, N. S. B2Y 2X3
Tel: 902 466 6691

India

Christian Meditation Centre
1/1429 Bilathikulam Road
Calicut
673006 Kerala
Tel: 495 60395

Ireland

Christian Meditation Centre
4 Eblana Avenue
Dun Laoghaire, Co. Dublin
Tel: 01 280 1505

Christian Meditation Centre
58 Meadow Grove
Blackrock, Cork
Tel: 021 357 249

Italy

Centro di Meditazione Cristiana
Abbazia di San Miniato al Monte
Via Delle Porte Sante 34
50125 Firenze
Tel/Fax: 055 2476302

New Zealand

Christian Meditation Centre
P.O. Box 35531
Auckland 1310

Philippines

5/f Chronicle Building Cor. Tektite Road
Meralco Avenue / Pasig
M. Manila
Tel: 02 633 3364
Fax: 02 631 3104

Singapore

Christian Meditation Centre
9 Mayfield Avenue
Singapore 438 023
Tel: 65 348 6790

Thailand

Christian Meditation Centre
51/1 Sedsiri Road
Bangkok 10400
Tel: 271 3295